Dear Tom

Thank you for the great picture that graces this book. When I asked you to "match" a 20 year old picture I laughed — but you did it. Thank you for being a great person + a caring family man — we hope to inspire more men like you. Warmly,

Elaine Parke

JOIN
—— THE ——
UNIVERSAL
𝔊olden
𝔕ule

REVOLUTION

Practice...
One Habit Each Month of the Year

ELAINE PARKE - Author

DARLENE PATRICK - Illustrator

CARING MEDIA
INTERNATIONAL

JOIN THE GOLDEN RULE REVOLUTION

Practice One Habit Each Month of the Year

Copyright © 2000 by Elaine Parke

Grateful Acknowledgements:
Cover Design   Darlene Patrick
Page Layouts and Design   Darlene Patrick
Type Design and Typography   Darlene Patrick
Quotation Research   Kaaren Radecki
Photographer   West Photography, Zelienople, PA
Fortune Cookie Philosophies   Ty Ling Fortune Cookie Company
Golden Rule Excerpts   Jeffrey Moses, *Oneness*, Fawcett, Columbine 1989
Quotations   Multi-sourced from many great hearts around the world,
                                      old and young, past and present.

INTERNATIONAL STANDARD BOOK NUMBER
ISBN 0-9677460-0-0

SELF-HELP	Happiness	SEL016000
	Motivational	SEL02100
FAMILY & RELATIONSHIPS	Interpersonal Relations	FAM027000
	Mores	FAM031000

LIBRARY OF CONGRESS CATALOG NUMBER
LCCN   00-190199

ATTENTION: If you are interested in quantity discounts, or would like to use sales of this book as an organization fund raiser, or if you can't afford this book but would like to have one, you may call 724-453-0447 or e.mail allofus@icubed.com or visit our website: www.goldenrulerevolution.com or write to Caring Media, 305 Furnace Drive, Suite B, Zelienople, PA 16063

 **CARING MEDIA** INTERNATIONAL

Caring Media International, Ltd.
305 Furnace Drive, Suite B, Zelienople, PA 16063-9719
Phone/FAX: 724-453-0447 e.mail: allofus@icubed.com
Website: www.goldenrulerevolution.com

UNIVERSAL
GOLDEN RULE

Treat others the way you would like them to treat you.

MUTUAL RESPECT

We have committed the Golden Rule to memory;
– let us now commit it to life.

AUTHOR UNKNOWN

DEDICATION

To George O. Parke
who gave unconditional love to me and to everyone
– even when it was difficult. He was a man well-loved
by legions of friends and family. He set the Golden Rule
example for all of us to follow and he did it easily.
Most of us have to work harder at it than he did.
His motto was service above self.
Thank you.

— And —

To All Children
everywhere.

*We have not inherited the earth from our ancestors,
we are borrowing it from our children.*

AUTHOR UNKNOWN

Dear Reader,

YOU and I together, can change our own lives and the world - starting right now. Thoughts become powerful beyond measure, when they reach lots of people at the same time and are repeated over and over again. Whether it's the death of a princess, a school tragedy in Colorado, or Nike, or Coke, or McDonald's; each of these thoughts is powerful because it is a common awareness shared by all of us at the same time.

By reaching many people at the same time we can create our own common awareness, and make it powerful beyond measure. It will only take a few of our moments each day. I have started this Golden Rule Revolution, because it is the beginning of a new millennium. It's time to create common awareness and make progress about the one thing we haven't gotten much better at – US!

You don't have to be a rocket scientist to know what to do. We have known how to live a kind, caring, and meaningful life for many millenniums. We have always known the Golden Rule is the greatest universal idea. As an idea rather than as a widely practiced action, however, it hasn't done us much good. It's time to make both the idea and the practice of the Golden Rule powerful beyond measure.

The Golden Rule is a guiding standard more than a specific "do-able" action. By practicing 12 easily do-able monthly Golden Rule qualities, we can make kindness and mutual respect powerful beyond measure. Whatever month it is, whatever day it is, take this book home with you and start now! Enjoy the daily refreshments of nourishing quotes and ideas that I have prepared for you.

Keep going. Day after day, month after month, year after year, until just like the Holidays, we will all together be practicing the same Habit of Golden Rule Living at the same time. Imagine someday, when March's Habit, "Resolve Conflicts," or April's Habit to "Take Care of Our Environment," will be celebrated in your home, your workplace and in your community. We will have converted the Golden Rule into actions that are practiced by more of us, all together, than ever before in history.

Doing the right thing is easy to say and more difficult to do, or we would have done better at it before now. This GOLDEN RULE REVOLUTION will work because we will support one another, by thinking about and increasing our own practice of the same monthly habit at the same time. One month is the length of time psychologists say it takes to turn actions into habits. Together, we will make the Golden Rule a year-round Habit that is powerful beyond measure.

Begin today, as I try to do, to nourish and reinforce your own practice of each monthly Golden Rule Habit more often. Commit to reading each daily Habit Reminder in this book, and to practice each month's Golden Rule Habit. Let the monthly caring colors be your "cues" for happiness. Share the monthly Habits with others – START A REVOLUTION of your own. Help regenerate the presence of Golden Rule Living among all those you know and love.

Together we can brighten the world we all share...

Elaine Parke

P.S. If I seem to be repeating myself, remember, that's how habits are formed! Welcome to the GOLDEN RULE REVOLUTION. I'm glad you are here.

JOIN THE GOLDEN RULE REVOLUTION
Practice One Habit Each Month of the Year

TABLE OF CONTENTS

FOREWORD *by Melvin H. Steals, Ph.D.*

INTRODUCTION — *A Five-minute Guide to this Book*

                                   Color - Gentle Aqua
I offer my habit to Lend a Hand
With 31 Small Acts of Kindness
Happy New Year!
What better way to start off your NEW YEAR
....than by Lending a Hand

                                   Color - WOW! Fuschia
I say to myself, You Count
With 28 Personal Confirmations
Happy Valentine's Day!
You make a difference on Valentine's Day and everyday!

                                   Color - Peaceful White
I strengthen my habit to Resolve Conflicts
With 31 Time-Out Suggestions
Happy Saint Patrick's Day!
It's spring! Make a fresh start by resolving conflicts.

Before the good fortune that brought Elaine Parke into my middle school building, it was one of the most violent and lowest performing middle schools in the Commonwealth of Pennsylvania. No one, including this principal, was safe from physical assault. This was due in no small part to the pervasion of a pernicious street culture and the widespread belief among the students that few of their teachers truly cared about them. It was at this point that Elaine appeared upon the scene.

The adjective that best describes the effect that she engendered is angelic. She unleashed a powerful tidal wave of positive emotion within our midst that we had never before experienced. In short, her Caring Habit of the Month Adventure program not only had a profoundly positive impact upon the feeling tone within the building, it also caused everyone who came into our school to be more caring about each other.

I have seen firsthand and personally experienced the chaos that has invaded many of our nation's schools. Elaine Parke's clearly defined prescriptions for positive change significantly reduced the fear that used to make learning so difficult within my middle school. I would highly recommend her book, The GOLDEN RULE REVOLUTION to everyone, and her Caring Habit of the Month Adventure program to any school district that has any concerns about operating a safe and orderly learning environment.

Melvin H. Steals, Ph.D.

The GOLDEN RULE is UNIVERSAL

The most important statement I want to make in this entire book – is that every single person is welcome here. I want you to know that you are valued, honored and respected for who you are and for whatever your beliefs are.

There are many great and glorious books about beliefs and faiths, but this is NOT one of them. This book is about the Golden Rule, as a helping tool for getting along with one another better and for living a happier, more meaningful life. I have a deep personal faith of my own, but my own beliefs are not what I am sharing with you in this book. This book is about sharing the practical Golden Rule truth that seems to be common among all beliefs.

> *The world cannot always understand a person's profession of faith, but it can understand service.*
> IAN MACLAREN

What makes the Golden Rule the best messenger for getting along with one another is it's basic common sense, that has been spoken in all languages and printed in all great religious books. It is not only a cornerstone of religious understanding, it is the epitome of COMMON SENSE. The practical effectiveness of Golden Rule actions can apply for agnostics and atheists, as well as for believers, from any religious point of view.

> *It is best to change the world on the basis of love of mankind, but if that quality be too rare, then common sense seems to be the next best thing.*
> BESSIE HEAD

Throughout this book I have attempted to represent a broad assortment of contributions, as fairly as I could. Where quotations have used male references, I have added notations to include the female reference. There may be opinions here that you do not share and which I hope you will respect. I will appreciate hearing from you with your own opinions and suggestions.

The Golden Rule reflects a common ethic that transcends the narrow confines of sectarianism. The oldest known and preserved Golden Rule message is believed to have come from the Sumerian Sun God "Utu" in 2350 BC. The God "Utu" was renamed "Shamash," after the Babylonians invaded and took over Mesopotamia.

> *Whatever has breath, you shepherd equally,*
> *You are their keeper, above and below.*
> SUN-GOD UTU

With appreciation to Jeffrey Moses from his book, *"Oneness,"** I am sharing with you some quotations (listed alphabetically), from great religious books of the world that reflect the universal wisdom of the Golden Rule.

BUDDHISM: *One should seek for others the happiness one desires for oneself. Hurt not others with that which pains yourself.*

CHRISTIANITY: *From the New Testament of the Bible, Matthew 7:12. "So in all things, do unto others what you would have them do unto you, for this sums up the law and the prophets."*

CONFUCIANISM: *Tzu-Kung asked: "Is there one principle upon which one's whole life may proceed?" The Master replied, "Is not Reciprocity such a principle? What you do not yourself desire, do not put before others."*

HINDUISM: *This is the sum of all true righteousness. Guard and do by the things of others as they would do by their own. This is, the sum of duty; do naught to others which if done to thee would cause thee pain.*

ISLAM: *Let none of you treat his brother in a way he would himself dislike to be treated. No-one of you is a believer until he loves for his brother what he loves for himself.*

JUDAISM: *What is hurtful to yourself, do not do to your fellow man. That is the whole of the Torah and the remainder is but commentary.*

*Moses, Jeffrey, *Oneness*, New York, Fawcett Columbine Books 1989

Why turn the universal principle of the Golden Rule into a more frequently practiced habit for yourself?

Because in its stark simplicity, the Golden Rule is more than a universal truth. It holds much of the answer to life's question, *"What's the point?"* We know when we practice qualities that result in harmonious relationships, that life has joy and wonder and depth. When I act with compassion I know I am more than a physical bag of skin with some gooey stuff in it.

The Golden Rule, is a "standard of behavior" more than it is a specific rule of behavior. To practice the Golden Rule you have to interpret it for yourself and translate its "do unto others" standard into whatever specific response is needed for each situation.

> *Caring moments well spent become caring moments well lived.*
> MARQUIS OF HALIFAX

The twelve (12) Monthly Habits are a way to make the Golden Rule easier to act on in our daily lives. It converts the Golden Rule into twelve actions, or habit-forming messages, that can be specifically interpreted and then acted on. These actions are each linked to a month because, like brand names, we already know the names of the months. In this format the names of the months and the monthly colors become "cues" to help us to remember each Golden Rule Habit.

> *We are what we repeatedly do.*
> *Excellence then, is not an art but a habit.*
> ARISTOTLE

The twelve (12) sets of Daily Inspirations in this book are the heart of the GOLDEN RULE REVOLUTION. The monthly celebration of these habits is the way we can all come together, at the same time, in common thought and practice. These pages are your HANDBOOK and your own personal "daily reminder system" to help you convert the Golden Rule into a more enriched and fulfilled life.

> *Civilization is just the slow process of learning to be kind.*
> WILL AND ARIEL DURANT, THE LESSONS OF HISTORY

DAILY HABIT-BUILDING INSPIRATIONS

A Habit-forming Golden Rule Reminder System for each day, each week, each month and all year long, year after year.

> *Practicing the Golden Rule is not a sacrifice,*
> *it's an investment.*
>
> BYLLE AVERY

What you have in your hand, is more than a book. It is a year-long, year-round, habit-forming Golden Rule reminder system, broken into the twelve months, and the twenty-eight to thirty-one days of each month. It is well known among psychologists, that it takes twenty-one to thirty days to form a habit. One month is just about the right length of time to repeat one thought and action, enough to form or strengthen an existing habit.

With this book you are about to launch on a great adventure – an adventure of re-inspired kindness and compassion that can grow and sustain you in your daily life. The fabric of this adventure is woven, not from new ideas, but from the time-honored wisdom of our shared experience that mutual respect between people is necessary for peace and fulfillment.

This is the first time a systematic plan, with materials to inspire you to remember and practice the Golden Rule has been developed using the months as habit-building units. On the following pages are 365 days of heartwarming quotes, poems, anecdotes, and action tips for Golden Rule living.

You may say, *"What is different about this inspirational book? There are many books like that."* The difference between this inspirational daily guide and others, is that all of the materials for each day are different. BUT – all of the materials for a single month are about practicing the same habit of the Golden Rule for the whole month. This book is about forging random acts of kindness into caring habits. Since habits take twenty-one to thirty days to form, you will strengthen your Golden Rule Habits while you move through time.

The 12 Monthly Habits are a way to make the Golden Rule easier to act on in our daily lives. Even when we feel we already treat other people well, most people would still like to improve. Most of us certainly wish OTHER people would improve and we believe that our families, our neighborhoods, our communities and the world would be better if we all practiced the Golden Rule more often.

With this book and a few minutes of your attention a day, you will strengthen your ability to convert values and qualities of the Golden Rule into personal daily habits. You will live through each year, from now on, by anchoring each month on one aspect of Golden Rule living. Your loving spirit and your daily thoughts and actions will become more in harmony with one another than ever before.

> *The good habits you cultivate*
> *put your dreams within your reach.*
> AUTHOR UNKNOWN

As you begin this adventure, you are joining many other people who are all together – celebrating life and building the GOLDEN RULE REVOLUTION, by practicing the monthly habits at the same time that you are. Their Golden Rule adventures are happening in their homes, their communities, their schools, their work places and places of worship. In one city, these monthly habit reminders have reached a million households each day as 30-second television spots. In another city, nearly 4,000 public school students experience these nourishing caring habit reminders every day and every month.

Soon, whenever you hear January, or see the color "cue" Aqua, you will immediately think, "Lend a Hand," the month to work on giving and compassion for others. You may go out of your way to help a neighbor with an ill relative, while someone in another city may pass out cookies and coffee to a work crew in their neighborhood. When you see or hear May, you will not only think Grateful Pink and Mother's Day, but you will also think about all the people and aspects of your life that you cherish and appreciate.

When you see or hear December, and see a beautiful EVER-Green tree, you will think not just about the long list of gifts you have to buy, but also about being patient with the store clerks while you shop. When your see or hear March, you will think of "peaceful white" the color of a lamb that represents peace. Perhaps soon, that March white lamb will be visiting street gang territories in our cities or visiting countries and places where conflict and war have torn apart the lives of millions.

> *Human brotherhood* is not just a goal. It is a condition on which our way of life depends. The question for our time is not whether all men are brothers. The question is whether we have the strength and the will to make the brotherhood of man the guiding principle of our daily lives.*   * *and sisterhood*
>
> JOHN F. KENNEDY, 35TH PRESIDENT OF THE UNITED STATES

Finally, you have in your hand, a way to transcend the confusion of ideas and the stress of wanting to be better, but not knowing how or where to start. I have found comfort in realizing that I am not alone in this ridiculous human crisis; it includes us all and has been here for thousands of years.

I've often thought that one of the reasons disasters bring out the best in people is because suddenly, there is no confusion. Our caring compassion is immediately tapped, because what to do becomes profoundly clear........... and we DO it. This easy year-round celebration of Golden Rule living also makes what to do and when, easy to do and easy to follow. All you need is the desire.

> *Readers are of two kinds –*
> *the reader who carefully goes through a book*
> *and the reader who lets the book go through him.*
> DOUGLAS JERROLD

The next 365 days, organized into 12 months of Golden Rule Adventure, is a journey prepared for you, and me, and others to follow. Each month not only has its own Golden Rule Habit and its own caring color "cue," it also has its own flavor and personality that has been designed to highlight the thought behind the attribute. There are little jokes in November when we celebrate "Show a Positive Attitude," and short "time-outs" for March while we practice "Resolve Conflicts." There are "praise phrases" to express appreciation in May, and short biographies of people who have "done their best" in September.

Remember, this is not a book of new ideas. This is a book about a new systematic way to reach out to all of us and join us together to improve our personal lives and our shared experience. When you use the monthly bookmark every day and read the Daily Inspirations, and plan "habit" actions for yourself, you are actually "surrounding yourself" with the message just like the media surrounds us with ideas and images. The difference is that you are choosing the idea and you are choosing to surround yourself with it, and make it more of a habit for yourself. YOU, not the media, are in charge of how you motivate your choices.

Practice makes permanent.
DR. DONALD SHEFFIELD
PROFFESSOR AT PENN STATE UNIVERSITY

Remember that every Golden Rule Habit is appropriate to practice ANY time of the year. Don't be afraid to repeat yourself, repetition is what helps form habits. Welcome to the GOLDEN RULE REVOLUTION. I'm glad you are here.

A LITTLE HISTORY

Perhaps you are interested in knowing how the Golden Rule Habits came about, and why each month was chosen to celebrate that habit. It all began nearly ten years ago, when I became inspired with the idea to designate each month of the year as a period of time to celebrate one aspect of Golden Rule Living. At the time, I was the Director of Marketing for a resort near a small town of about thirty thousand people in southwestern Pennsylvania. This community was the first town that got together and tried out the infant idea.

A group of community people became interested and met together each month to work on how the Golden Rule Habits plan would work. The group included the Mayor; the Chief of Police; the Director of the County Welfare Office; the Chairman of the Ministerial Association, the Superintendent of Schools; the Executive Director of the local Chamber of Commerce; the owner of a local printing company; the owner of the local radio station; and students from the local high school plus other residents, neighbors, volunteers and friends.

At the first meeting of this group, I shared the format I had in mind – to celebrate a different aspect of Golden Rule living each month. For nearly a year they met, to compose the Golden Rule Habits and select which month in which to celebrate each habit. The Golden Rule Habits in this book are the outcomes of the spirit and dedication of a group of people, who represented every perspective and every aspect of any community. It was a pure community endeavor – reflecting the perspective of everyone. For me, every day will always be a "Be Appreciative" day when I think of this dedicated group of people who lent their spirits, their minds and their hearts to build the foundation of what you have in your hand today. Thank you, everyone.

We all agreed back then, and you probably do too, that the habits we settled on -- could have been different. There were many long discussions and much chafing and then bonding of hearts and minds. Maybe you would have included a Golden Rule Habit that we didn't or you would have put one in a different month than this system does.

However, step back for a minute with me, and look at the big picture. If you and I, and other people, start practicing these habits every day, then soon, each month, all month long, our lives will become more like the Golden Rule standard. It will be kind of like turning around a parade - if you turn it around at a few strategic points, the rest will turn too. Ultimately, it won't matter exactly which Habit is celebrated in which month, as much as it matters that we all agree and share the same experience at the same time.

In the late 1990's, a large insurance company in Pittsburgh funded the development of a Golden Rule project to help middle school students reduce bullying and violent behaviors. This is when I met Dr. Melvin Steals. At that time, we added a monthly color "cue" system to improve recognition and retention of each habit for all the students. The school program is called, "The Caring Habit of the Month Adventure."

GOLDEN RULE HABITS and MONTHLY COLORS

Here are the Golden Rule Habits, with a short explanation about how and why each was chosen and identified with its month. One of the things you'll notice is that the school year, holidays, and the northern hemisphere seasons are important considerations. I hope our friends in the southern hemisphere will understand, and will agree to practice these habits anyway.

The color "cues" are a wonderful support system for helping each of us remember to practice the Golden Rule Habits. In our school curriculum program, The Caring Habit of the Month Adventure, we call them our "Caring Colors." Each of the colors has its own special name, that sort of fits the theme of the month. Each color helps us to remember the Golden Rule Habit it signifies.

Even though the book begins with JANUARY and ends with DECEMBER, you do NOT have to start in January. You can START RIGHT NOW!! Just find the week and the day and BEGIN. Each chapter is filled with daily inspirations that include quotes, meditations and special tips. Even though each day's inspirations are different, all of the inspirations for one month are about the same Golden Rule Habit, so that by the end of the month you have strengthened your own habit. Each month is introduced with some inspiration and motivation to get us started.

> *Motivation is what gets you started.*
> *Habit is what keeps you going.*
>
> JIM RYUN, AMERICAN LONG DISTANCE RUNNER

MONTHLY HABITS and COLORS

JANUARY   *Golden Rule Habit*   **Lend a Hand**
                  Monthly Color   Gentle Aqua

"Lend a Hand" is celebrated in January, because right after the holiday season the spirit of good will just ends abruptly. In many areas, January is a cold dark month, when many people need help too. It seemed practical to keep the holiday mood going in January, by promoting the Golden Rule Habit to "Lend a Hand." "Gentle Aqua" is a color to remind us of compassion and caring for others.

FEBRUARY *Golden Rule Habit*   **YOU Count**
          Monthly Color   WOW! Fuchsia

"You Count" was selected for February because its holiday, Valentine's Day, is a day to celebrate the importance of others in your life and to be celebrated by them. WOW! Fuchsia is a color that stands out in a crowd, just like we all do. In the United States we also celebrate February as "Black History Month." The idea "You Count" expands on the meaning of Black History to include a celebration of every one and of every ethnic history.

MARCH   *Golden Rule Habit*   **Resolve Conflicts**
          Monthly Color   Peaceful White

"Resolve Conflicts" is a new way to interpret the old adage, "March comes in like a lion and goes out like a lamb." A lamb is usually white and so is the sign of peace, the color "Peaceful White." When you resolve any lingering conflicts in your life, you turn your own lions into lambs no matter what the weather is. St. Patrick's Day also reminds us of the country of Ireland, which has had one of the longest running conflicts in recent history.

APRIL   *Golden Rule Habit*   **Take Care of Our Environment**
          Monthly Color   Spring Green

"Take Care of Our Environment," was chosen for April, because Earth Day is celebrated on April 21. In the northern hemisphere, April is a spring month, when the budding of trees and flowers are natural reminders that our earth needs our love and care to nourish our future and our children. Think spring, the color "Spring Green," that is. In April many organizations in communities everywhere have celebrations and events to promote stewardship of our planet.

MAY   *Golden Rule Habit*   **Be Appreciative**
          Monthly Color   Grateful Pink

"Be Appreciative," is a perfect Golden Rule Habit for the Month of May. May has Memorial Day, Mother's Day and is the month when teachers, government service workers and many volunteers across

America are honored and appreciated for all they do. Think pink this month. "Grateful Pink" is for Mom and for all those you appreciate each day.

JUNE	*Golden Rule Habit*	**Get Out of a Rut**
	Monthly Color	JOLT! Orange

"Get Out of a Rut" is celebrated in June because it's the end of the school year and the beginning of summer. It's a great month to "break routine," and plan an interesting vacation, or start something to improve yourself. Its a time for creativity and dreams of change and renewal. "JOLT! Orange" is a color to grab your attention and get you out of your routine.

JULY	*Golden Rule Habit*	**Become Involved**
	Monthly Color	Patriot Red

"Become Involved" is what America's founding fathers did when they felt they could create a better life for the early colonists. Good citizenship is more than just voting. July is a great month to give meaning to your 4th of July Celebration by volunteering your time to a cause that is important to you. "Patriot Red" is just the color to encourage you to do it!

AUGUST	*Golden Rule Habit*	**Know Who You Are**
	Monthly Color	Thoughtful Blue

"Know Who Your Are" is something we often don't take time to think about. August is usually hot and a good time for vacations. Vacations are a good time for reflection. Our color this month, "Thoughtful Blue," is soft and quiet to support "taking stock" of you.

SEPTEMBER	*Golden Rule Habit*	**Do Your Best**
	Monthly Color	Award Gold

"Do Your Best," is a perfect Golden Rule Habit for September, when the new school year really gets underway. A do your best frame of mind is the best way to start right and to make commitments that will insure a good job at whatever you do. September's color rewards our hard work with "Award Gold."

OCTOBER   *Golden Rule Habit*   **Be Patient & Listen**
                  Monthly Color   Slow-down Lavender

"Be Patient & Listen" was a Habit our group felt was important to practicing the Golden Rule. October seemed like a good month to focus on these qualities because this month and this habit were left when we worked out the other months. Our great October color, "Slow-Down Lavender," really sets the mood.

NOVEMBER *Golden Rule Habit*   **Show a Positive Attitude**
                  Monthly Color   Sunny Yellow

"Show a Positive Attitude" is the Golden Rule Habit for November, because it includes the quality of Thanksgiving and because it is a great frame of mind for going into the holiday season of December. "Sunny Yellow" is a color that reminds us of the famous smiley face that is a well know symbol everywhere.

DECEMBER   *Golden Rule Habit*   **Celebrate Community,**
                                             Family & Friends
                  Monthly Color   EVER-Green

"Celebrate Community, Family & Friends" wraps up the year and captures the essence of what the holiday season is all about, no matter what religious belief you hold. The color EVER-Green is a reminder that it is family and friends, and community that are the abiding and enduring aspects of a fulfilling life. Practicing the Golden Rule is a way to keep it all together during the rough spots.

The MONTHLY REMINDER BOOKMARKS

Your Habit-building reminder bookmarks at the back of this book are helpful tools for increasing your ability to work on each month's habit. The color of each bookmark provides you with an extra "reminder cue" for its own special month. When you see each color anywhere, think about its special Golden Rule Revolution name, like "Ever-Green" or "Peaceful White" or "Grateful Pink." Remind yourself about what each of these colors stands for. Tear out each bookmark and use it in this book and/or other books during the entire month.

You can add to your bookmark reminders by making other reminders of your own to put in easily seen places in your home or place of work. You can make a desk topper, kitchen table or work area reminder, (like they put on restaurant tables), and other small "reminder signs" to tape to your bathroom mirror or on the phone or even on the dashboard of your car. If you are a computer user, you can create monthly screensavers to remind you (and others in your home or office) of each month's Golden Rule habit.

At the back of this book is also a *Reply Card* to register as a Golden Ruler, a *Golden Ruler Card* to carry in your wallet, a *12 Habits of the Golden Rule Bookmark*, and a *Sign* to place somewhere handy to remind yourself to stay committed.

Someday we will all be sharing something at the same time – but it won't be a war or a disaster, or even a Coke break. Together we will be sharing the year-round habit of practicing the Golden Rule.

"Together We Can Brighten the World We All Share."

Speak with care,
Your words become actions,

Act with care,
Your actions become habits.

Repeat an act with care,
Your habits become character.

Form your character with care,
Your character becomes your destiny.

JIM RYUN
SEEN ON THE WALL AT SIR SPEEDY PRINTING COMPANY

CHAPTER 1

LEND A HAND™

in **January** and All Year Long!

Color "Cue" - Gentle Aqua

"Together We Can Brighten the World We All Share."

16

IN JANUARY, REMEMBER TO...
LEND A HAND

January is the beginning of a fresh new year and a great time to carry on the spirit of holiday giving. This month, when you see the color aqua, "Gentle" Aqua, that is, think of how valuable you are, and know that you can help others each day – even with a smile.

Perhaps you have made your New Year's resolution; and perhaps not. Either way, I want to start your year by sharing with you, one of the loveliest treasures I have found on this GOLDEN RULE REVOLUTION journey. I am presenting it to you as a "January Promise." There is a place for you to sign this Promise.

THE JANUARY "LEND A HAND" PROMISE*

I promise to be tender with the young,

Compassionate with the aging,

Sympathetic with the striving,

And tolerant with the weak and the wrong...

Because sometime in my life I will have been ALL of these!

My Signature_____

This Date_____

*The words of this "Promise", allegedly from an unknown contributor, were printed in the Washington Post many years ago. They are a rare gift of the spirit to all of us. Thank you.

Goal for the Month:

To lift our spirit and the spirits of others
by caring and sharing and giving.

"Together We Can Brighten the World We All Share."

Do all the good you can,

By all the means you can,

In all the ways you can,

In all the places you can,

At all the times you can,

To all the people you can,

As long as ever you can.

JOHN WESLEY

TODAY...   *I offer my habit to*
LEND A HAND

You have begun your new year by lending a hand to yourself. THANK YOURSELF, for taking time to read a small part of this book every day. Appreciate yourself for being determined to make the GOLDEN RULE more active in your life than ever before. This short poem is a great "reminder" and a compass for daily thinking.

> *To look up and not down, to look forward and not back;*
> *to look out and not in, and to lend a hand.*
>
> EDWARD EVERETT HALE, AMERICAN AUTHOR, "TEN TIMES ONE IS TEN"

Plan to hold a "Lend a Hand" party this month. You might ask everyone to bring an item of food for the needy and to bring their own stories about helping others and about being helped.
Notice the mood of the evening.
Isn't it great?? !!

𝔊𝔬𝔩𝔡𝔢𝔫 𝔑𝔲𝔩𝔢 Habit

In January
LEND A HAND™

1
January
2

TODAY...   *I offer my habit to*
LEND A HAND

We live in an "over-busy" world where, like horses with blinders, our "to-do" lists prevent us from noticing the needs of others around us. Stopping to be helpful takes just minutes from our day, the joy received is timeless.

> *If you stop to be kind, you must swerve often from your path.*
> MARY WEBB, PRECIOUS BANE

> *Happiness is the by-product of helping others.*
> DENNY MILLER

Be watchful today, for someone who needs your help
and a bit of your time.

TODAY . . .   ***I offer my habit to***
LEND A HAND

Life is little things. Think about what pleased you yesterday. Did a co-worker smile as you passed in the hall? Did you find a flower bud, or a new sprout on one of your house plants? Did you get an unexpected hug at home?

> *Life is not so short but that there is always*
> *time enough for giving courtesy.*
>
> RALPH WALDO EMERSON, AMERICAN POET AND ESSAYIST

The difference between a helping hand
and an outstretched palm is a twist of the wrist.

LAWRENCE LEAMER, AMERICAN AUTHOR, KING OF THE NIGHT

Leave a cookie or other treat and a note of thanks for your newspaper or mail delivery person.

3
January

4

In January
LEND A HAND™

𝔊𝔬𝔩𝔡𝔢𝔫 ℜ𝔲𝔩𝔢 Habit

TODAY . . .   ***I offer my habit to***
LEND A HAND

Life happens in little moments. You have power over how they add up. Think about each moment today. Live today by making a memory and a treasure out of each moment.

> *Little deeds of kindness,*
>   *Little words of love*
> *Help to make earth happy*
>   *Like the heaven above.*
>
> JULIA A. FLETCHER CARNEY, 'LITTLE THINGS'

In this world, you must be a bit too kind in order to be kind enough.

PIERRE CARLET DE CHAMBLAIN DE MARIVAUX

Give a parking break – let someone in ahead of you with a smile.
Give a smile and a thank you to every store clerk who helps you today.

TODAY . . . ***I offer my habit to***
LEND A HAND

We are powerful spiritual beings meant to create good on the earth. This good isn't usually accomplished in bold actions, but in singular acts of kindness between people. It's the little things that count, because they are more spontaneous and show who you truly are. I am elated. I now know the simple secret to improving mankind. The amount of love and good feelings you have at the end of your life is equal to the love and good feelings you put out during your life.

DANION BRINKLEY, AUTHOR - SAVED BY THE LIGHT
(SURVIVED THE "LONGEST MEDICAL DEATH" ON RECORD)

Surely there is some "singular act of kindness" in your heart,
at this minute, that you can do for another.
– Hug your child, or your spouse, or a friend.
Only you know.

Golden Rule Habit — In January LEND A HAND™ — January 5 / 6

TODAY . . . ***I offer my habit to***
LEND A HAND

What is wisdom? How wise are we as we begin a new millennium of time? What kind of progress have we made toward equality and justice for all? Are you wise? What does progress mean to you?

Civilization is just the slow process
of learning to be kind.

WILL DURANT

Kindness is more important than wisdom,
and the recognition of kindness is the beginning of wisdom.

THEODORE ISAAC RUBIN, M.D., PHYSICIAN & AUTHOR, ONE TO ONE

Tell your bus driver how much you appreciate his or her driving.
Perhaps your "bus driver" is your spouse, or your mom or dad,
or your older brother or sister, or a volunteer.

TODAY... **I offer my habit to**
LEND A HAND

As you go through your day, pay special attention to the people you interact with. If you notice someone is irritable or evasive or aloof – try to look for a reason to feel compassion rather than criticism or blame.

> *Two important things are to have a genuine interest in people*
> *and to be kind to them. Kindness, I've discovered,*
> *is everything in life.*
>
> ISAAC BASHEVIS, SINGER, JEWISH-AMERICAN AUTHOR

> *There's more power in the open hand than in the clenched fist.*
>
> MARTIN LUTHER KING, JR.

Today I will give a note to someone offering to help them.
I already know who needs this note from me.

7
January
8

In January
LEND A HAND

Golden Rule Habit

TODAY... **I offer my habit to**
LEND A HAND

How do you make a living?

> *From what we get, we can make a living;*
> *what we give, however, makes a life.*
>
> ARTHUR ASHE, AMERICAN TENNIS PLAYER, DAYS OF GRACE

> *You've got to give to get.*
> *And if you don't plan on givin',*
> *then you better not plan on gettin'.*
>
> JOE CLARK

Be a buddy or friend to a new co-worker, a new neighbor,
or a new student at school. Show them you notice them.
Express a genuine interest in learning about them.

TODAY . . .   *I offer my habit to*
LEND A HAND

What is success?

> *Success has nothing to do with what you gain in life*
> *or accomplish for yourself. It's what you do for others.*
> DANNY THOMAS, ACTOR-COMEDIAN

You roll my log, and I will roll yours.
SENECA INDIAN SAYING

> *We're not primarily put on this earth to see through*
> *one another, but to see one another through.*
> PETER DEVRIES, LET ME COUNT THE WAYS

Before you go to bed tonight, write down on paper your own definition of success. Think, during the day, about what success means in your life and what you hope to leave as your legacy someday.

In January
LEND A HAND

𝔊olden 𝔑ule Habit

9

January

10

TODAY . . .   *I offer my habit to*
LEND A HAND

People need our help and so does our environment, and our plants, and animals. "Lend a Hand" to our birds and other animals. I have a friend who once said, "Help everyone and if your can't help, at least don't hurt them." We can help, by not hurting our environment.

> *You give but little when you give your possessions.*
> *It is when you give of yourself that you truly give.*
> KAHLIL GIBRAN

We must decide how we are valuable rather than how valuable we are.
EDGAR Z. FRIEDENBERG

Hang a bird feeder – and keep it filled. Give treats to your own pet or one to someone elses – even if the treat is only a pat or a hug of affection. Make a contribution to save the habitat of an endangered species.

TODAY . . .   *I offer my habit to*
LEND A HAND

Joy is a gift you give to yourself and others.
Even if you have troubles and you don't feel like it
– fake it for a while and see what happens.

Give a smile and good cheer to everyone you see
– from the moment you open your eyes in the morning
until you close them again at night.

Smiles are wondrous things;
you can give them out for eternity
and still have one left for yourself.
COLLEEN, AGE 13 - FROM "THE PEANUT BUTTER GANG"

11*
January

In January
LEND A HAND™

A smile is
——the beginning of peace.
MOTHER TERESA

Hum a few tunes today.
Here are several songs you may know.

Put on a Happy Face   *from Bye Bye Birdie*

When You're Smiling   *Judy Garland, Performer*

Service with a Smile   *Cheryl Prewitt-Salem*

Zip-a-Dee-Do-Dah   *from Song of the South*

*Today is my own birthday.
Smiles and Joy and Music are my favorite things.

TODAY . . . I offer my habit to
LEND A HAND

I read somewhere that the healing power of prayer has been scientifically proven. No matter what you believe, try sending positive prayers or thoughts to someone you know who is experiencing pain or grief.

Kindliness antedates psychiatry by hundreds of years;
it's antiquity should not lessen your opinion of its usefulness.
DR. J. ROSWELL GALLAGHER

Make yourself necessary to somebody.
RALPH WALDO EMERSON

If you have an elderly neighbor, check-in on them today.
Pray for them, that their needs will be met.
Who else needs your prayers today?

In January
LEND A HAND™   **12**

𝕲𝖔𝖑𝖉𝖊𝖓 𝕽𝖚𝖑𝖊 Habit   January

13

TODAY . . . I offer my habit to
LEND A HAND

Spend today acknowledging how other peoples' lives are intertwined with your own. Look around you. Ask yourself who made the chair you're sitting on. Think about who picked the potato you're having for dinner. Think about who stocked the shelves at the grocery store.

We seldom stop to think how many peoples' lives are entwined with
our own. It is a form of selfishness to imagine that every one can operate
on his own or can pull out of the general stream and not be missed.
IVY BAKER PRIEST, GREEN GROWS IVY, FORMER UNITED STATES TREASURER

A friend in need is a friend in deed.
QUINTRAS ENNIUS

Write a note to a person from your past who intertwined their life with yours when you needed it most. Give them a gift of your appreciation.

TODAY . . . ***I offer my habit to***
LEND A HAND

One of my observations is that we try to substitute words for actions when it comes to making a better world. Sometimes we talk a good line when it comes to telling others what to do but the question is, *"Do 'we' walk the talk?"*

> *Words are plentiful, but deeds are precious.*
>> LECH WALENSA, FORMER POLISH PRIME MINISTER LEADER OF "SOLIDARITY"

> *The impersonal hand of government can never replace the helping hand of a neighbor.*
>> HUBERT H. HUMPHREY, FORMER VICE PRESIDENT OF THE UNITED STATES

TODAY: Walk the talk. Remember the three "R's" – Respect for self; Respect for others; Responsibility for all your actions.

14
January
15

In January
LEND A HAND™

𝔊𝔬𝔩𝔡𝔢𝔫 𝔕𝔲𝔩𝔢 Habit

TODAY . . . ***I offer my habit to***
LEND A HAND

Happiness is the by-product of helping others.
>> DENNY MILLER

> *If I can stop one heart from breaking,*
> *I shall not live in vain.*
> *If I can ease one life the aching,*
> *Or cool one pain,*
> *Or help one fainting robin unto his nest again,*
> *I shall not live in vain.*
>> EMILY DICKINSON, AMERICAN POET

Lend the hand of gratitude.
Thank your spouse, child, parent, friend, boss, secretary, or teacher for the things they do and have done for you.

TODAY . . .   *I offer my habit to*
LEND A HAND

Practicing random acts of kindness became popular because giving became an "event" – a series of great and wonderful surprises. There used to be a tradition practiced at the gates of Grateful Dead concerts. People would buy an extra ticket and give it to a "ticket-in-need" stranger standing outside the gate. This "tradition" was called "miracling."

> *The love we give away is the only love we keep.*
>> ELBERT HUBBARD, NOTE BOOK

> *God speaks wherever He finds a humble, listening ear.*
> *And the language He uses is kindness.*
>> LENA HORNE, SINGER-ACTRESS

Give a stranger a ticket to a
sports event or concert.

Golden Rule Habit

In January
LEND A HAND™

16
January
17

TODAY . . .   *I offer my habit to*
LEND A HAND

Nourishment is easily recognized when it is offered in the form of food. Words and caring stories are nourishment, too. Maybe this is why the inspirational book *Chicken Soup* is so popular. Food as nourishment is a symbol of caring for one another. This is what we do when a family loses a loved one, or when there is illness, or simply to welcome the arrival of a new baby or a new neighbor.

> *Who gives to the poor gives to God.*
>> VICTOR HUGO

> *We must strive to multiply bread*
> *so that it suffices for the tables of mankind.*
>> POPE JOHN PAUL II

Bring a large batch of your "best recipe" home-made cookies to a homeless shelter. Offer to volunteer.

TODAY... ***I offer my habit to***
LEND A HAND

Show everyone you meet today that you care about them. While you are with them – a clerk at a store, a co-worker with a problem, a child with a bad attitude – let them know you think they are important and valuable people.

> *People want to know how much you care*
> *before they care how much you know.*
> JAMES F. HIND, THE WALL STREET JOURNAL

> *Friendship is the pleasing game of interchanging praise.*
> OLIVER WENDELL HOLMES, AMERICAN AUTHOR

Actually say the words, "I care about you," to someone.

18
January
19

In January
LEND A HAND

𝔊𝔬𝔩𝔡𝔢𝔫 𝔯𝔲𝔩𝔢 Habit

TODAY... ***I offer my habit to***
LEND A HAND

Do you have charity in your heart today? Share your heart full of charity. Invite someone to join you in attending your place of worship, or a service organization, where you know there is warmth and caring.

> *If you haven't any charity in your heart,*
> *you have the worst kind of heart trouble.*
> BOB HOPE, ACTOR-COMEDIAN

> *A real friend is...*
> *one who helps us think our best thoughts,*
> *do our noblest deeds, and be our finest selves.*
> AUTHOR UNKNOWN

Give people more than they expect and do it cheerfully.

TODAY . . .   I offer my habit to
LEND A HAND

Look for the secret that sparks joy, and motivates someone you love.
Ignite that spark with your words or your actions.

Every human being has some hand by which he may be lifted, some
groove in which he was meant to run; and the great work of life, as far
as our relations with each other are concerned, is to lift each one by
his own proper handle, and run each one in his own proper groove.

HARRIET BEECHER STOWE, AMERICAN AUTHOR, "LITTLE FOXES"

The entire sum of existence
is the magic of being needed by just one person.

VI PUTNAM, HARD HEARTS ARE FOR CABBAGE

Live a good and nourishing life. Then when you get older
and think back, you'll get to enjoy it twice.

In January

LEND A HAND™

20

𝖦𝖔𝖑𝖉𝖊𝖓 𝖱𝖚𝖑𝖊 Habit   January

21

TODAY . . .   I offer my habit to
LEND A HAND

Expect a miracle today. Look in the mirror. Hold up your hand. Look
carefully at your own face and your own hand. YOU are the miracle.
Surely there is a miraculous kindness that you can bestow on another.

The miracle is this —
the more we share, the more we have.

LEONARD NIMOY, ACTOR

When friends ask me when the (Quaker) service is
— I tell them that service comes after the (Quaker) meeting.

WILLIAM PENN, FOUNDER OF PENNSYLVANIA

You can give the gift of laughter today.
You are a miracle.
If you know a joke, tell it to someone who needs a joke.

TODAY . . .   *I offer my habit to*
LEND A HAND

Look through today's local newspaper headlines. Notice stories where people have been hurt or sustained a loss. Think about how you would feel had this happened to you. Consider doing something to help. Call the newspaper, TV station, or the police, to find out what you can do.

> *A community is not a place. It begins in thought, and lives in the heart and spirit. Community is in the climate of empathy.*
> ELAINE PARKE

> *The worst prison would be a closed heart.*
> POPE JOHN PAUL II

Give the tools of courage to someone who needs it
– perhaps someone whos story is in the newspaper.

22
January
23

In January
LEND A HAND™

𝕲𝖔𝖑𝖉𝖊𝖓 𝕽𝖚𝖑𝖊 Habit

TODAY . . .   *I offer my habit to*
LEND A HAND

Call or contact someone today you don't "think" you like very well. Convey a compliment or a positive message. If you feel awkward at first, tell them you think they have great elbows or that you know they keep a very neat medicine chest. I'm sort of kidding a little bit, but you get the point.

The heart is the toughest part of the body. Tenderness is in the heart.
CAROLYN FORCHE, THE COUNTRY BETWEEN US

> *The only thing we can offer of value is to give our love to people as unworthy of it as we are of God's love.*
> ST. CATHERINE OF SIENNA

At the end of the day, ask yourself how you now feel about the person you contacted.

TODAY . . .   I offer my habit to
LEND A HAND

Really LOOK at your HAND today. Hold it open. Imagine giving.
Feel the warmth of knowing that you care.

> *There was a man, though some did count him mad.*
> *The more he cast away, the more he had.*
> JOHN BUNYAN

> *The best place to find a helping hand is at the end of your arm.*
> ELMER LETERMAN

> *A hand up is better than a hand out.*
> SYBIL MOBLEY

Watch your own hand give a cookie to a child
or a cup of coffee to a co-worker.

In January
LEND A HAND™

24
January
25

Golden Rule Habit

TODAY . . .   I offer my habit to
LEND A HAND

Write a "satisfaction" letter, (instead of a "complaint" letter) to the
boss of an employee or to someone who has helped you. Imagine being in the room when the boss tells this employee he/she has received
your letter. What do you think the boss will say? How do you think the
employee will feel?

> *I hope, when I stop, people will think that somehow I mattered.*
> MARTINA NAVRATILOVA, WOMEN'S TENNIS CHAMPION

> *Shall we call ourselves benevolent,*
> *when the gifts we bestow do not cost us a single privation?*
> DEGERANDO

Write a note to your spouse or a loved one. You know what to say.

TODAY...   ***I offer my habit to***
LEND A HAND

On a rainy day, share the shelter of your umbrella with someone who doesn't have one. Go a little out of your way if need be. If it's too cold for rain where you live this time of year, help someone with a weather hazard in another way. I'm sure you'll think of something.

I expect to pass through life but once. Therefore, if there be any kindness I can show, or any good I can do for any fellow-being, let me do it now, and not defer or neglect it, as I shall not pass this way again.

WILLIAM PENN, FOUNDER OF PENNSYLVANIA

Service is the rent you pay for room on this earth.

SHIRLEY CHISOLM, FORMER UNITED STATES CONGRESSWOMAN

Do someone else's job at home tonight – preparing dinner, washing the dishes, taking the garbage out, putting the kids to bed...

26

January

27

In January
LEND A HAND

𝕲𝖔𝖑𝖉𝖊𝖓 𝕽𝖚𝖑𝖊 Habit

TODAY...   ***I offer my habit to***
LEND A HAND

Not what we give, but what we share –
For the gift without the giver is bare;
Who gives himself with his alms feeds three –
himself, his hungering neighbor, and me.

JAMES RUSSELL LOWELL, AMERICAN POET

The manner of giving is worth more than the gift.

PIERRE CORNEILLE

Give what you have.
To someone it may be better than you dare think.

HENRY WADSWORTH LONGFELLOW, AMERICAN POET

Take a plate of tasty cookies or a cheerful plant
to the police or fire department.

TODAY... *I offer my habit to*
LEND A HAND

If you haven't used it in two years, then give it away. Have you ever seen a U-Haul truck in a funeral procession? Have you ever seen the happy face of a child, on a cold day, with a new coat?

> *No one may forsake his neighbor when he is in trouble.*
> *Everybody is under obligation to help and support his*
> *neighbor as he would himself like to be helped.*
> MARTIN LUTHER

One can give nothing without giving oneself — that is to say, risking oneself. If one cannot risk oneself, then one is incapable of giving.
JAMES BALDWIN, AMERICAN AUTHOR

Can you risk giving away something – that maybe – sorta –
– somehow – you're not sure – but even though you haven't used it lately – you just might need again
– some day?

In January
LEND A HAND™

28

<u>**Golden Rule Habit**</u>   January

29

TODAY... *I offer my habit to*
LEND A HAND

What would happen to "road rage" if all drivers were courteous and kind to one another? Give another driver a good parking spot that you saw before they did. Notice the look on their face when they realize what you are doing. Later in the day, let someone pull in front of you who is waiting to enter an intersection.

> *One can never pay in gratitude, one can only pay "in kind"*
> *somewhere else in life...*
> ANNE MORROW LINDBERGH, NORTH TO THE ORIENT

> *Kindness consists in loving people more than they deserve.*
> JOSEPH JOUBERT

Plan to be a courteous driver today – again tomorrow
– and again, the day after that – and after that.

TODAY...   *I offer my habit to*
LEND A HAND

It's almost the end of January, but not the end of the need to help and support each other. Perhaps this month, you've become re-acquainted with how brief... and simple... and non-eventful... and normal... the real essence of giving can be. You can give away a million dollars, an hour of your time, or just a smile. Each of these gifts is important.

> *Dedicate some of your life to others. Your dedication will not be a sacrifice. It will be an exhilarating experience because it is an intense effort applied toward a meaningful end.*
>
> DR. THOMAS DOOLEY, AMERICAN MEDICAL MISSIONARY

> *Find out where you can render a service, and then render it.*
>
> S.S. KRESGE, AMERICAN MERCHANT

Make a pledge to keep your
giving spirit going.

30

In January
LEND A HAND™

January

Golden Rule Habit

31

TODAY...   *I offer my habit to*
LEND A HAND

Tomorrow, we start experiencing the Golden Rule Habit reminder, "You Count." Remember that you "count" when you lend a hand to others. Opportunities to help others are as small and effortless as a smile. Keep your hand open and the thought "Lend a Hand" in your heart as you begin the month of February and the new monthly habit "You Count."

> *He who waits to do a great deal of good at once, will never do anything.* SAMUEL JOHNSON

> *Great opportunities to help others seldom come, but small ones surround us every day.*
>
> SALLY KOCH

Softly, to yourself, say the words, "peace begins with me."
I can give a smile that is heartfelt, spontaneous, and free.

CHAPTER 2

YOU COUNT™

*in **February*** *and All Year Long!*

Color "Cue" - WOW! Fuchsia

"Together We Can Brighten the World We All Share."

Give a gift of the *Golden Rule Revolution* to the people in your life.
For quantity pricing see the card at the back of this book. If someone else has used this form, you may
phone: 724-453-0447 e.mail: allofus@icubed.com or visit our website: www.goldenrulerevolution.com

IN FEBRUARY, REMEMBER THAT...
YOU COUNT

This month's celebration color is "WOW Fuchsia." Whenever I see the color "fuchsia," I will remember that I count and that I make a difference wherever I go. "I Count" is a feeling of worth, the sense of having value, the knowledge that you are good and have the power to do good. In February, we celebrate Black History Month and Valentine's Day. Both of these celebrations honor the value of each of us in the lives of others.

To know that you count means knowing that you have a purpose and that you have personal gifts to fulfill that purpose. HOW do we count? How do we feel self-worth and personal value? By using our own resources, we use:

Our time... Our thoughts... Our energy.

We make decisions every day that affect our lives and the lives of others. We determine our own lives and influence others by living our own dreams, not by following someone else's. We are not all the same. This is what is so exciting about being alive. Imagine how boring the world would be if we really were all the same. Imagine if every person you met was blond with brown eyes, or was wearing a white Polo shirt or a brown pair of oxford wing-tip shoes?

All of us together is the essence of community. Each one of us COUNT!! A farmer, a doctor, a teacher, a carpenter; they all provide some necessary ingredient needed for the community to operate properly. They all count. In our homes and in our community, we all play a role in the group activity. We can all do things that count and feel joy and success in life.

Making a difference doesn't have to be a big deal. Look around you. Look at the paper clip you may use sometime today to hold several sheets of paper together. Somebody made that paper clip! For you, that person counts. If that person hadn't made the paper clip your papers would fall apart.

38

Survey your skills, your hopes and your dreams and write them down. Do you have a dream you keep secret because you don't believe it could ever happen? Let the Daily Inspirations work in your mind and in your heart this month. Re-dedicate yourself to you – and to those around you.

<u>Goal for the Month</u>:

To know that you count and to BELIEVE it.

"Together We Can Brighten the World We All Share."

1994 INAUGURAL SPEECH

"Our deepest fear is not that we are inadequate.
Our deepest fear is that we are powerful beyond measure.
It is our light, not our darkness, that most frightens us.

We ask ourselves,
Who am I to be brilliant, gorgeous, talented and fabulous?
–Actually, who are you not to be?"

NELSON MANDELLA, FORMER PRESIDENT OF SOUTH AFRICA

TODAY . . .   *I say to myself*
YOU COUNT

Today's quote, below, written by Booker T. Washington is one of my favorites. He understood that each one of us is important every moment of every day. We all have the ability to enrich and support one another or to tear one another down. Each day you are given a bank account of 1,440 minutes. No person on earth gets more than you do.

> *You've got to put your own bucket down*
> *where you are.*
> BOOKER T. WASHINGTON

Today I'll do "<u>good</u>"!

Golden Rule Habit   COU NT   February

Y
O
U
NT
in February

1

2

TODAY . . .   *I say to myself*
YOU COUNT

In the United States, February 2nd is Groundhog Day.
The groundhog, Punxsutawney Phil, from a little town in western Pennsylvania, counts! Legend has it that when Phil leaves his home in the ground today and sees his shadow, we're in for six more weeks of winter weather.

You make a difference – every day – no matter what the weather.

> *You need only claim the events of your life*
> *to make yourself yours.*
> FLORIDA SCOTT-MAXWELL, THE MEASURE OF MY DAYS

Today I'll be thoughtful and gentle with others.

40

TODAY... ***I say to myself***
YOU COUNT

Black History Month is dedicated to the idea that we all count–no matter what our history or what our beliefs are. This is a month to honor African Americans. Booker T. Washington founded the Tuskeegee Institute as a great contribution to our country. Together we all share the responsibility for building a better world. Even one smile helps someone.

Our flag is red, white, and blue, but our nation is a rainbow –
red, yellow, brown, black and white
– and we're all precious in God's sight.
REV. JESSE JACKSON

America is not a melting pot – America is a beautiful mosaic.
PAT DERIAN

Today I'll read some Black History.

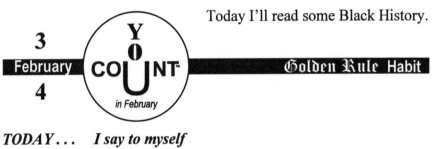

3
February
4

Golden Rule Habit

TODAY... ***I say to myself***
YOU COUNT

February is a wonderful month to remember that our children count too. "You Count" in the lives of children. If you have children at home, spend extra time with them or with your grandchildren or with the neighbor's children. Let children know you value and respect them. Encourage them to know they count.

Children don't learn...
from people who don't love them.
(THE LATE) GENERAL JOHN STAFFORD, SUPERINTENDENT - SEATTLE PUBLIC SCHOOLS

Give a little love to a child and you get a great deal back.
JOHN RUSKIN

Today I'll be patient with children.

TODAY . . . *I say to myself*
YOU COUNT

Becoming more self-reliant is another way to celebrate "You Count." Maybe you've wanted to learn more about handling your own finances or about calculating your taxes. Celebrate "You Count" by taking charge of a new aspect of your life.

> *You can count on others*
> *but it's better to use your own fingers and toes.*
> BAZOOKA JOE

> *Always do what you say you are going to do.*
> *It is the glue and fiber that binds successful relationships.*
> JEFFREY A. TIMMONS, THE ENTREPRENEURIAL MIND

Today I'll find out how to do it myself
and then do it.

Golden Rule Habit

Y
O
COUNT
U
in February

February

5

6

TODAY . . . *I say to myself*
YOU COUNT

We all have days when nothing seems to go right. Today, think about your own significance in the face of adversity. Whether it's your own or someone else's, you can be a part of the solution. For those who know they "count," the pains of living become the lessons of life.

> *Turn hurt into a halo, turn scars into stars.*
> REV. ROBERT SCHULLER, AMERICAN CLERGYMAN

> *There are victories of the soul and spirit.*
> *Sometimes, even if you lose, you win.*
> ELIE WIESEL

Today I'll make lemonade out of lemons.

TODAY... **I say to myself**
YOU COUNT

Who is the "YOU" that counts in this month of February? Take a few minutes to take stock. For a few days, you might even want to keep a journal. Write down the moments each day when you know you counted – when you gave encouragement to a friend, when you made a helpful suggestion at work, or when you listened to a child.

You never find yourself until you face the truth.
PEARL BAILEY, AMERICAN SINGER-ACTRESS

Not all of us have to possess earth shaking talent.
Just common sense and love will do.
MYRTLE AUVIL

Today I'll take ten quiet moments with me.

7

February

8

COU**NT**
Y O
in February

𝔊𝔬𝔩𝔡𝔢𝔫 ℜ𝔲𝔩𝔢 Habit

TODAY... **I say to myself**
YOU COUNT

Have you ever lost a small screw from a piece of equipment and found that the whole thing broke down? Just like a small screw, each one of us is holding something together in our own part of the world. As you go through your day, think about this at home with your family, at work, or just out in the community.

Everybody has to be somebody to somebody to be anybody.
MALCOLM S. FORBES, AMERICAN BUSINESSMAN

When we turn to each other, and not on each other,
that's victory.
REV. JESSE JACKSON

Today I'll call someone and ask them over to share a meal with me.

TODAY . . .   I say to myself
YOU COUNT

Random Acts of Kindness week is celebrated this month. Why is each of us important and unique? With your words and actions today, let the people around you know that you respect them and value their place in your life. Build them up – look at their point of view – show kindness regularly rather than randomly. Show that you care.

Commandment Number One of any truly civilized society is this:
Let people be different.
DAVID GRAYSON

Life is rather like a can of sardines – we're all looking for the key.
ALAN BENNET

Today I'll tell each person
why they are valuable to me.

Golden Rule Habit   **Y O U COUNT** in February   **9**   February   **10**

TODAY . . .   I say to myself
YOU COUNT

Do you ever feel small and unimportant?
I know I do. This is the month to remember that every person is important. Each of us is needed by someone every day. How rich or how powerful we are is not a measure of importance. However, in today's society we lose sight of this. What is the measure of importance in your life?

Even a small star shines in the darkness.
FINNISH PROVERB

There is not enough darkness in the world
to put out the light of even one small candle.
ROBERT ALDER

Today I'll find value in each thing I do.

44

TODAY . . .   *I say to myself*
YOU COUNT

February is American Heart Month.

One way to show yourself that "You Count"
is to focus on your own health.

Are there some bad habits, like smoking, that you would like to break?

Are there some heart-healthy habits you can improve like choosing
more nutritious foods, exercising more and taking more time to relax?

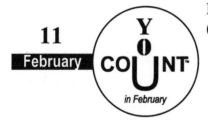

11
February

Repeat this quote several times today
(and everyday):
>*I am a Promise.*
>*I am a Possibility.*
>GLORIA & WILLIAM GAITHER

Here is some "healthy" advice from Heather Dixon,
a 4th grader in Bethel Park, Pennsylvania.

H *elp other people*
E *xercise regularly*
A *void guns and violence*
L *earn safety rules*
T *ake time to rest*
H *andwashing often*
I *llegal drugs and alcohol are bad*
E *at healthy foods*
R *espect nature*

Today, I'll enjoy this humor...
It's all right to drink like a fish if you drink what a fish drinks.

TODAY . . .   *I say to myself*
YOU COUNT

Today is Abraham Lincoln's Birthday.

> *Common-looking people are the best in the world:*
> *that is the reason the Lord makes so many of them.*
> ABRAHAM LINCOLN, 16TH PRESIDENT OF THE UNITED STATES

I sort of flinch at the concept of "common-looking people." Who wants to look common? However, maybe Abe was onto something when he realized the truth about what is really important in life. From now on, I will regard "common-looking" as a badge of distinction.

Today I'll observe the people I see
with a new respect for who they are.

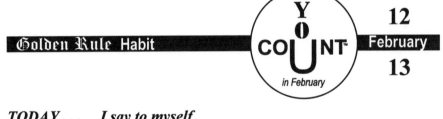

Golden Rule Habit   CO**U**NT   **February**

12

13

Y**O**U COUNT in February

TODAY . . .   *I say to myself*
YOU COUNT

There are those who march to a different drummer in a parade all their own. Many of us step out onto paths others will not first take – but upon which others will soon follow. Who is your drummer? Be courageous enough to stay on a course that you believe in and to follow your own truth. You Count.

> *How glorious it is – and how painful also – to be an exception.*
> ALFRED DE MUSSET

> *If a man does not keep pace with his companions, it is perhaps*
> *because he hears a different drummer. Let him step to the music*
> *that he hears, however measured or far away.*
> HENRY DAVID THOREAU, AMERICAN AUTHOR

Today I'll take a different path home.

F
E
B

TODAY ...   *I say to myself*
YOU COUNT

Love is the ultimate expression of "You Count." On Valentine's Day, we celebrate and honor love. Saint Valentine's Day was originally the Roman feast of Lupercalia. It was Christianized in memory of the martyr St. Valentine (d. A.D. 270). In the Middle Ages, Valentine became associated with the union of lovers under conditions of duress. Today, the holiday is celebrated with the exchange of romantic or comic messages called "Valentines."

The supreme happiness of life is knowing we are loved.
VICTOR HUGO, FRENCH AUTHOR, LES MISERABLES

Today I'll call or send Valentine greetings to everyone I can.

14 February — **Y O U COUNT** *in February* — 𝔊𝔬𝔩𝔡𝔢𝔫 ℜ𝔲𝔩𝔢 Habit
15

TODAY ...   *I say to myself*
YOU COUNT

You probably have a few Valentine's cards in your home today. Valentine's Day is such a great day of the year for bolstering our own sense of self worth. Really cherish the cards you received this year. Think about the verses written on them and cherish the people who sent them to you. Immerse yourself in love.

No one can figure out your worth but you.
PEARL BAILEY

Everybody is somebody.
JESSE JACKSON

Today I'll make myself some cookies and then share them.

TODAY...   *I say to myself*
YOU COUNT

Today, prove to yourself that you count. Count the number of minutes you have in a 24 hour day. Do you realize that time is the ultimate equalizer? Did you come up with 1,440 minutes like I did? How many times can you make a difference in 1,440 minutes? Have you ever realized that there is no one on earth who has more minutes each day than you do?

> *What we must decide is how we are valuable*
> *rather than how valuable we are.*
> EDGAR Z. FRIEDENBERG

> *You have '1,440 POWER,' today and every day,*
> ELAINE PARKE

Today I'll call someone and share
something positive about today.

Golden Rule Habit   Y O COUNT U NT *in February*   February   **16**   **17**

TODAY...   *I say to myself*
YOU COUNT

We all count in this world, for better or for worse. We don't mean to cause "worse" – yet sometimes, even without knowing it, our words or actions hurt others. I remember the childhood ditty "sticks and stones." One way adults hurt each other is with gossip. Make a commitment today to stay away from gossip.

> *Sticks and stones may break our bones,*
> *but words will break our hearts.*
> ROBERT FULGHUM

> *Frogs have it easy, they can eat what bugs them.*
> AUTHOR UNKNOWN

Today I'll make a commitment to stay away from all gossip
– even if someone bugs me.

TODAY . . . **I say to myself**
YOU COUNT

Trust is a secular word for faith. When you have self-trust, you have faith and confidence in yourself and what you have to give to others. Self-trust is basic to the concept of "You Count." Go forth into your day with faith and trust.

> *Self-trust is the essence of heroism.*
> RALPH WALDO EMERSON, AMERICAN AUTHOR AND POET

> *Trust yourself, then you will know how to live.*
> JOHANNES WOLFGANG VON GOETHE

Today I'll remember to trust myself when I am tempted to please someone else against my own better judgment.

18
February · **COUNT** · in February · ☙olden Rule Habit
19

TODAY . . . **I say to myself**
YOU COUNT

Remember those 1,440 minutes that you now know you have today? Like ants on a log, each minute seems tiny compared to large measures of time like the millennium. Think about a project you want to do that is overwhelming. Today, imagine that project is a pile of bricks that you place, one by one, into a structure that is the success you are looking for. It is beautiful, isn't it?

> *It is the greatest of all mistakes to do nothing*
> *because you can only do a little.*
> *Do what you can.*
> SYDNEY SMITH

Today I'll start something I've been putting off.

TODAY...   *I say to myself*
YOU COUNT

Here is a story about four people. Their names are
– Everybody, Somebody, Anybody and Nobody.

> *There was an important job to be done and*
> *Everybody was sure that Somebody would do it.*
>
> *Anybody could have done it, but Nobody did it.*
>
> *Somebody got angry about it because it was Everybody's job.*
>
> *Everybody thought Anybody could do it,*
> *but Nobody realized that Everybody wouldn't do it.*
>
> *It ended up that Everybody blamed Somebody,*
> *when Nobody did what Anybody could have done.*

Today I'll be the one who does the job.

Golden Rule Habit

Y
O
CO U NT
in February

20
February
21

TODAY...   *I say to myself*
YOU COUNT

Step back from your day for a moment – look at how all the unique
people of the world work together to make things bloom and grow.
You are one of all of us. The gift of you and your uniqueness adds to
the life we share.

> *You are unique, and if that is not fulfilled,*
> *then something has been lost.*
> MARTHA GRAHAM, AMERICAN DANCER

> *I make the most of all that comes and the least of all that goes.*
> SARA TEASDALE, "THE PHILOSOPHER"

Today I'll write myself a complimentary note
and post it where I can see it quite often.

50

TODAY . . .   *I say to myself*
       YOU COUNT

This is George Washington's Birthday. The strength of our democracy is based on this month's Caring Habit. "You Count." Do you honor your democratic responsibility to vote? What special rights do you have as a democratic citizen? Here is a reminder from the Declaration of Independence.

> *We hold these truths to be self-evident;*
> *that all men are created equal; that they are endowed by*
> *their Creator with unalienable rights; that among these are*
> *life, liberty and the pursuit of happiness.*
>
> THE DECLARATION OF INDEPENDENCE

Today I'll take inspiration from George Washington
and dedicate it to the tasks I need to accomplish in my own life.

22
February
23

Y
CO**U**NT
O
in February

𝔊𝔬𝔩𝔡𝔢𝔫 ℜ𝔲𝔩𝔢 Habit

TODAY . . .   *I say to myself*
       YOU COUNT

Why is it so difficult to be a friend to yourself? I know sometimes, I'm afraid to speak up for myself because I want to be liked. Today let's both work on speaking up for ourselves with courage and conviction – knowing that our friendship with ourselves is the basis for our friendship with others.

> *Be a friend to yourself, and others will be so, too.*
> THOMAS FULLER

> *Our entire life, with our fine moral code and our precious freedom,*
> *consists ultimately in accepting ourselves as we are.*
> JEAN ANOUILH

Today I'll be kind to myself and form the basis for improvements from acceptance of myself as I am.

TODAY...   *I say to myself*
YOU COUNT

I read a quote that I can't remember exactly, but it was something like
"Make memories today that you can live with tomorrow
– and for the rest of your life."
What profoundly good advice. Imagine how we all would behave, each moment, if we really thought about the memories we would be left with tomorrow.

Each of us is the accumulation of our memories.
ALAN LOY MCGINNIS, THE ROMANCE FACTOR

The best thing you can give your children
are good values, good memories and good food.
AUTHOR UNKNOWN

Today I'll spend quality time with a child.

Golden Rule Habit   **YOU COUNT** in February   **24** February **25**

TODAY...   *I say to myself*
YOU COUNT

If we look at the BIG picture and realize that there is a place in it for each of us – then we have no choice but to be ourselves. If we were someone else – then there wouldn't be anyone to fill our place. You are the only person who can be you. If you decide to be another "them" instead of "you" – your place will be left empty. Only you, being YOU, can fill your place and your shoes.

Be yourself. Who else is better qualified?
FRANK J. GIBLIN II

We must be our own before we can be anothers.
RALPH WALDO EMERSON

Today I'll value myself with a bubble bath or a bouquet of flowers.

TODAY . . .   *I say to myself*
YOU COUNT

Look for the signs people wear. Behind each person's words
and deeds are signs that tell us who they are and
what is important to them. All children wear the sign:
'I want to be important now.' Many of our juvenile-delinquency
problems arise because nobody read the sign.

DAN PURSUIT

To put yourself in another's place requires real imagination,
but by so doing,
each Girl Scout will be able to live among others happily.

JULIETTE LOW, FOUNDER, GIRL SCOUTS

Today I'll be more aware of who others really are
and of how they may view life from inside their hearts.

26
February
27

COUNT   𝔊olden 𝔑ule Habit

TODAY . . .   *I say to myself*
YOU COUNT

February is almost over. If there is one aspect of "You Count" that is
most important – it is knowing that "you" make a difference every
single minute of the 1,440 minutes you have to spend each day.

Tomorrow is the most important thing in life.
It comes into us at midnight very clean.
It's perfect when it arrives and it puts itself in our hands.
It hopes we learned something from yesterday.

JOHN WAYNE

You never get a second chance to make a first impression.

HEAD AND SHOULDERS TV COMMERCIAL

Today I'll buy some colorful balloons to celebrate me.

TODAY . . .   *I say to myself*
YOU COUNT

You Count. A caring habit is a form of memory that guides your actions toward the possibility that you make a positive difference today and every day. Remember, this is only one of the 1,440 minutes you own today. How will your habits guide you to use the other 1,439?

> *You are a memory and a promise.*
> *I am a promise. I am a possibility.*
> GLORIA AND WILLIAM GAITHER

> *We're all in this leaky boat together.*
> ROBERT OLDENSKI

Today I'll commit to my 1,400 POWER,
every day of the year.

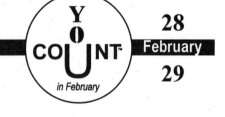

Golden Rule Habit — **Y O U COUNT** *in February* — **28 February 29**

TODAY . . .   *I say to myself*
YOU COUNT

Every four years
I have an extra day for me.

I will use it well.

I count.

CHAPTER 3

RESOLVE CONFLICTS™

*in **March** and All Year Long!*

Color "Cue" - Peaceful White

"Together We Can Brighten the World We Share"

Give a gift of the *Golden Rule Revolution* to the people in your life.
For quantity pricing see the card at the back of this book. If someone else has used this form, you may
phone: 724-453-0447 e.mail: allofus@icubed.com or visit our website: www.goldenrulerevolution.com

IN MARCH, REMEMBER TO...
RESOLVE CONFLICTS

In February, we focused on individual worth and self-esteem. Individual efforts can do quite a bit to change the world around us, but we can do so much more if we resolve conflicts and work together.

Ann Landers once suggested that we observe a National Reconciliation Day. As part of the GOLDEN RULE REVOLUTION, we have one whole month to do that – this month of March.

The celebration color for March is "Peaceful White." "WHITE" is the color of truce and also the color of a lamb. I have looked for information about how white came to be the color of truce and haven't found it yet. Perhaps you, one of my readers, will find it for me.

The first day of spring is in March and we begin to look for warmer weather. Our "climate," however, is composed of much more than the weather. We create our "habit-tat" with our habits and attitudes. More than anything else, whether or not the sun is shining, you determine the climate of your day.

Even if you begin this month like a lion, decide to go out like a lamb. Think about St. Patrick's Day and the terrible conflicts that families have endured in Ireland. Send them your prayers and wishes for peace and healing.

During this month, work on your relationships. We all would like to strengthen our bonds with co-workers, family and friends. This is the month to do it. Take time to resolve conflicts you have had with others. Lighten up; give a little; compromise. You will be happier and healthier for the effort.

Resolving conflicts with someone that you disagree with takes a lot of courage, and this is the time to begin. Start with a smile and begin "mending fences." I've included a copy of the Official Mediation Process used by professional mediators in business and legal situations.

Take a moment to read through it. You may find it helpful for you now, or perhaps, in the future.

Pick up the phone or write a letter one day this month. Take a few extra minutes with someone who gives you problems. Try to learn more about their point of view. Life is too short to hold grudges. Forgiving others is a great feeling. Reach out today, perhaps right in your own home.

Goal for the Month:

Patch up a relationship with at least one person.

"Together We Can Brighten the World We All Share."

The Mediation Process
Resolve Conflicts by Knowing the Steps for Mediation

I. Introduction

1. Introduce yourself as a mediator. Ask someone to write down the answers to the questions you will be asking the participants.
2. Ask those in the conflict if they would like your help in solving the problem. Do not proceed unless both parties agree.
3. Find a quiet area to hold the mediation.
4. Ask for agreement to the following:
   ____ try to solve the problem
   ____ no name calling
   ____ let the other person finish talking
   ____ confidentiality

II. Listening

5. Ask the first person, "What Happened?"
6. Ask the first person how (s)he feels.
7. Ask the second person, "What Happened?"
8. Ask the second person how (s)he feels.

III. Looking for Solutions

9. Ask the first person what (s)he could have done differently.
10. Ask the second person what (s)he could have done differently.
11. Ask the first person what (s)he can do here and now to help solve the problem.
12. Ask the second person what (s)he can do here and now to help solve the problem.
13. Use creative questioning to bring disputants closer to a solution.

IV. Finding Solutions

14. Help both disputants find a solution they feel good about.
15. Repeat the solution and all of its parts to both disputants and ask if each agrees.
16. Congratulate both people on a successful mediation.

The Resolving Conflicts RAP

ARNIE MCFARLAND, WRITTEN FEBRUARY 17, 1992

Sometimes there's a reason for the way you feel,
Cause somebody's made you mad.
>*And there are times when someone is mad at you.*
>*Hey, you know that you've been bad.*

Well all of us know that for the month of March,
If we take the first step and try,
>*To end the fight between them and you,*
>*You might get a big surprise.*

If you forgive them and they forgive you,
You'll feel like a brand new day.
>*Resolving conflicts takes away stress.*
>*Come on! Try it the Golden Rule way.*

In the month of March it's "take the first step."
You know you can do it too.
>*Resolving conflicts isn't easy,*
>*But there's something in it for you.*

TODAY . . . I strengthen my habit to
RESOLVE CONFLICTS

Today, look for the lions of conflict and anger that are in your life now. Who are you on the "outs" with – who are you not getting along with? Where are the relationships that need resolution and healing before peace will come?

Here is an excellent guideline:
> *When a person forgives another, he is promising to do*
> *three things about the intended wrongdoing–*
> *First: not to use it against the wrongdoer in the future;*
> *Second: not to talk about it to others; and*
> *Third: not to dwell on it himself.*

JAY ADAMS

Today: Walk away!

1
March

Golden Rule Habit

2

TODAY . . . I strengthen my habit to
RESOLVE CONFLICTS

Peace is a key to happiness at every level of life – personally, in the family, in the community, in schools, in businesses, in countries and throughout the world. This month of March, "Let there be peace on earth and let it begin with me."

> *For it isn't enough to talk about peace.*
> *One must believe in it.*
> *And it isn't enough to believe in it.*
> *One must work at it.*

ELEANOR ROOSEVELT, FORMER FIRST LADY

> *Violence is a one way street to nowhere.*

AUTHOR UNKNOWN

Today: Count to ten.

62

TODAY . . . **I strengthen my habit to**
RESOLVE CONFLICTS

There are people in our lives who are just plain hard to get along with. A realistic solution, in these situations, is to let your problems with them roll off your own back. Take a few minutes to chuckle at the humor of today's quote. However, in keeping with the spirit of the GOLDEN RULE, I'm suggesting that you never, never think of another person as a pig.

> *Never get in a conflict with a pig.*
> *You'll both get muddy and the pig will enjoy it.*
> CALE YARBOROUGH, AMERICAN AUTO RACER

Laughter changes our perception of pain: physical and emotional.
BOB BASSO, PH.D.

Today: Laugh!

3
March
4

RESOLVE
CONFLICTS™
in March

𝔊𝔬𝔩𝔡𝔢𝔫 𝔎𝔲𝔩𝔢 Habit

TODAY . . . **I strengthen my habit to**
RESOLVE CONFLICTS

Have you ever met a person who builds up their own throne
with bayonets?

In daily life one of the bayonets people use against each other is sarcasm. Sarcasm can be used to win arguments and to put people down. Do you know what it feels like when people use sarcasm against you? How can you reduce the use of sarcasm in your own life?

> *You can build a throne with bayonets;*
> *but you can't sit on it for long.*
> BORIS YELTSIN, PRESIDENT OF RUSSIA

Today: Love.

TODAY ...   *I strengthen my habit to*
RESOLVE CONFLICTS

We all know we don't like to be angry and that anger is stressful. It's so easy to forget what anger does to us, while we're caught up in what we're doing to the other person. What we may not realize, is that anger draws our mind and our energies from meaningful tasks at work and at home. What does it take for you to let go of your anger and give yourself the freedom of a clear fresh mind?

> *Anger blows out the lamp of the mind.*
> AUTHOR UNKNOWN

> *Be angry but don't let the sun go down on your anger.*
> AUTHOR UNKNOWN

Today: Change your perspective on anger.
It's not good for you.

Golden Rule Habit — **RESOLVE CONFLICTS** in March — **5 March 6**

TODAY ...   *I strengthen my habit to*
RESOLVE CONFLICTS

Forgiveness is a key to resolving conflicts because it is the part that we can control. We can NEVER control the other person – only ourselves. We can never change other people – we can only change ourselves. If we feel we are wronged, we can't always get the other person to apologize, but we can be forgiving no matter what.

> *A good marriage is the union*
> *of two forgivers.*
> RUTH BELL GRAHAM, WIFE OF REV. BILLY GRAHAM

Today: Hold your breath for 10 seconds while you calm down.

TODAY ...   ***I strengthen my habit to***
RESOLVE CONFLICTS

Sometimes the best way to heal small conflicts is simply to change your own perspective. How big and how bad is the problem you are having with someone? Can you change your own perspective about it, rise above the problem and go on as if there were nothing really wrong?

> *I just read that one out of every four people is unbalanced.*
> *Try to think of three of your best friends.*
> *If all three of your friends seem balanced and all right to*
> *you, then you must be the unbalanced one.*
> SLAPPY WHITE, AMERICAN COMEDIAN

Today: Close your eyes and picture a beautiful scene
– a beach or a lush woodland.

7
March

8

RESOLVE CONFLICTS™
in March

𝕲𝖔𝖑𝖉𝖊𝖓 𝕽𝖚𝖑𝖊 Habit

TODAY ...   ***I strengthen my habit to***
RESOLVE CONFLICTS

"I need space." Have you ever said those words? Are you being truthful or stubborn? Are you fleeing from a problem with someone instead of finding the courage to find a common ground of agreement? I have done both and find that escape is seldom a real solution, only a short term gratification. Find a way to agree with someone and rise against the wind, even when it isn't easy.

> *"Birds in their little nests agree," he said. "So why can't we?"*
> JOHN STEINBECK, AMERICAN AUTHOR, THE WINTER OF OUR DISCONTENT

> *Don't be afraid of opposition.*
> *Remember, a kite rises against, not with the wind.*
> HAMILTON WRIGHT MABLE

Today: Find a common ground.

TODAY... *I strengthen my habit to*
RESOLVE CONFLICTS

Getting in the middle of a problem between others is considered risky business. Maybe it's because our words often becomes fuel for their fire. Try listening to a friend's complaints about another person with a true interest in helping them solve the problem. Work hard at not fueling their fire or adding to a chain of gossip.

> *My doctrine is this, that if we see cruelty or wrong*
> *that we have the power to stop, and do nothing,*
> *we make ourselves sharers in the guilt.*
> ANNA SEWELL, BRITISH AUTHOR, BLACK BEAUTY

Today: Bake a cake for a friend with a problem.

RESOLVE **9**
Golden Rule Habit **CONFLICTS** March
in March **10**

TODAY... *I strengthen my habit to*
RESOLVE CONFLICTS

Successfully using humor in a "resolve conflict" situation is a matter of timing, but it can be done. When anger is high, humor can be interpreted as a "belittling" lack of respect for the other person's point of view. Begin to resolve a conflict by listening and negotiating. Use humor later in the process to bring emotions back together into a renewed common bond that humor can help to strengthen.

> *Using humor is like changing a diaper:*
> *it's not a permanent solution,*
> *but it makes everybody feel better.*
> JEANNE ROBERTSON

Today: Find humor in whatever the situation.
Humor is always there somewhere.

66

TODAY . . . ***I strengthen my habit to***
RESOLVE CONFLICTS

I think love is the biggest and best four-letter word in the world. There is nothing love cannot face. There is no limit to love's faith, love's hope, and love's endurance. What do you think? Where can you give and receive more love in your own life?

> *What the world needs now is love, sweet love.*
> *It's the only thing that there's just too little of.*
> HAL DAVID, AMERICAN COMPOSER, "WHAT THE WORLD NEEDS NOW IS LOVE"

> *Love cures people, the ones who receive love*
> *and the ones who give it, too.*
> KARL A. MENNINGER, AMERICAN PSYCHIATRIST

Today: Spend time with someone you love.

11
March

12

RESOLVE CONFLICTS in March

𝕲𝖔𝖑𝖉𝖊𝖓 𝕽𝖚𝖑𝖊 Habit

TODAY . . . ***I strengthen my habit to***
RESOLVE CONFLICTS

Think about the words in your life
that have broken your heart.

Remember that angry words are often said as weapons rather than said as the truth. Today, let go of the hurts that come from angry words. You'll feel the freedom. Make a commitment not to use those words yourself in relationships with others.

> *Sticks and stones may break our bones,*
> *but words will break our hearts.*
> ROBERT FULGHUM

Today: Enjoy the beauty of a tree.

TODAY... ***I strengthen my habit to***
RESOLVE CONFLICTS

Tolerance is a value that we all know is vital to living in peace with our neighbors. It's a puzzlement, why we humans think other people have to be like us or think like us to be acceptable. We all know that life works because we are different and we each bring special gifts to life that enrich the world around us.

> *When we honor diversity, we have no enemies.*
> JANE HUGHES GIGNOUX

> *It is never too late to give up our prejudices.*
> HENRY DAVID THROEAU, AMERICAN AUTHOR

Today: Appreciate what is different.

𝕲𝖔𝖑𝖉𝖊𝖓 𝕽𝖚𝖑𝖊 Habit

RESOLVE CONFLICTS in March

13
March
14

TODAY... ***I strengthen my habit to***
RESOLVE CONFLICTS

Who wants to be wrong? I don't know anyone – do you? Today, think about someone you may not be getting along with right now. Is there some way that you can heal the relationship by taking more responsibility for what went wrong?

> *Two wrongs don't make a right*
> *—but two Wrights made an airplane.*
> AUTHOR UNKNOWN

> *Quarrels would not last long*
> *if only one party were in the wrong.*
> FRANCOIS, DUC DE LA ROCHEFOUCAULD

Today: Look into the other person's heart.

TODAY . . .   *I strengthen my habit to*
RESOLVE CONFLICTS

We've been strengthening our habit to "Resolve Conflicts" for two weeks now. There is a formal process used by professional mediators to resolve conflicts that anyone can follow. It is known as The Mediation Process and with permission, I have included it at the beginning of this chapter. There are 16 steps in the formal process. If you have not read it earlier, take the time now, or reread and refresh your memory.

> *There is always hope*
> *when people are forced to listen to both sides.*
> JOHN STUART MILL

Today: Commit to learning the Meditation Process. You may never use all of the steps but knowing the process can help in other ways.

15
March
16

in March

(Golden Rule Habit)

TODAY . . .   *I strengthen my habit to*
RESOLVE CONFLICTS

We live in such a fast-paced and complex world that even without a specific conflict with someone – it's easy to feel like we live in a battle zone. Our relationships can be part of our support system or part of our problems. What can you do today to be a support system for yourself and for others in your life?

> *There are enough targets to aim at*
> *without firing at each other.*
> THEODORE ROOSEVELT, 26TH PRESIDENT OF THE UNITED STATES

Today: Commit (again) to learning the Meditation Process.

TODAY . . .   *I strengthen my habit to*
RESOLVE CONFLICTS

Today is St. Patrick's Day. Conflict anywhere in the world is a choice.

> *Nothing is resolved by war. On the contrary,*
> *everything is placed in jeopardy by war.*
> POPE JOHN PAUL II, ADDRESS, ROME, 1992

> *If we can't teach our children that fighting is not the answer,*
> *then we failed – as parents and as human beings.*
> *So you can hit me, or you can shake my hand, the choice is yours.*
> JASON SEAVER, "GROWING PAINS"

> *Don't be a noble fighter, 'cause kindness is righter.*
> POPEYE, "THE POPEYE CARTOON SHOW"

Today: Choose peace, not conflict.

Golden Rule Habit

RESOLVE CONFLICTS *in March*

17
March
18

TODAY . . .   *I strengthen my habit to*
RESOLVE CONFLICTS

"Mend your fences" is an America idiom for the idea to "resolve con-flicts." This has always puzzled me. Why would you repair a fence between yourself and someone else? The idiom says to keep your fences mended and strong, instead of suggesting that you take them down. Think about any fences you may have in your life.
Is it time to take them down?

Father Taylor of Boston used to say:
> *'There is just enough room in the world for all the people in it,*
> *but there is no room for the fences which separate them.'*
> RITA SNOWDEN

Today: Contact someone and "mend" a fence.

TODAY... **I strengthen my habit to**
RESOLVE CONFLICTS

Sometimes we can resolve conflicts by educating ourselves about the other person in the conflict. Have you ever experienced anger and irritation from someone, only to learn later that they were dealing with a terrible problem in their own life that had nothing to do with you?

> *There are only two ways of changing men (people) – one is by education of spirit, mind, and body, and the other is by violence ...education is the one peaceful technique for creating changes for the better.* HOWARD H. BRINTON

> *Let us convince our children that carrying a book*
> *is more rewarding than carrying a gun.*
> AUTHOR UNKNOWN

Today: Talk yourself out of anger.

19
March
20

Golden Rule Habit

TODAY... **I strengthen my habit to**
RESOLVE CONFLICTS

We can't spend this month strengthening our "resolving conflicts" habit without paying some attention to "temper." In the last few years we've coined phrases like "road rage" to describe what happens when temper overtakes common sense and threatens even our physical safety behind the wheel of a car. Managing our own emotions takes courage and conviction. The easy way out is to blame the other person.

> *Hot heads and cold hearts never solved anything.*
> REV. BILLY GRAHAM, AMERICAN EVANGELIST

> *Courage is the price life exacts for granting peace.*
> AMELIA EARHART, AMERICAN AVIATRIX

Today: While driving, listen to soft music. Think peace.

TODAY . . . **I strengthen my habit to**
RESOLVE CONFLICTS

I found more quotes about forgiveness than about any of the other concepts that help us resolve conflicts in our lives.
Why is forgiveness so hard to do?
Think about someone who you believe has wronged you today.
What can you do to forgive them?
Where do you need forgiveness?

M
A
R

Forgiveness is of the highest value, yet its cost is nothing.
BETTY SMITH, AMERICAN AUTHOR, A TREE GROWS IN BROOKLYN

Life is an adventure in forgiveness.
NORMAN COUSINS, FORMER EDITOR, "SATURDAY REVIEW"

Today: Forgive someone. Forgive two people.

Golden Rule Habit   RESOLVE CONFLICTS *in March*   **21**
March
22

TODAY . . . **I strengthen my habit to**
RESOLVE CONFLICTS

I chuckle at myself when I think about how perfect I'd be if I had never made the same mistake twice. Sometimes we get into conflict with ourselves because we expect so much and feel like a failure when we let ourselves down. Mistakes and wrong-doings are not to be taken lightly, but harboring guilt is never the way to improve yourself or to make your life better.

Experience enables you to recognize a mistake
when you make it again.
FRANKLYN P. JONES

Forgive yourself. Then if you face a choice
to be right or to be kind, choose kind.
DR. ERNIE PANZA, CHIROPRACTOR AND NATIONAL SPEAKER

Today: Forgive yourself.

TODAY . . . **I strengthen my habit to**
RESOLVE CONFLICTS

During the height of the "peace movement" in the 60's, the Catholic Church had a great slogan, "If you want peace, work for justice." Sometimes we accuse our children unjustly when we don't know all the facts and react with our emotions instead of our hearts. Think about justice in your own life today. How can you be more caring and fair in your judgment towards others?

> *Injustice anywhere*
> *is a threat to justice everywhere.*
> MARTIN LUTHER KING, JR., LETTER FROM THE BIRMINGHAM JAIL, AUGUST, 1963

Today: Intentionally be just and fair with others in your life.

23
March
24

Golden Rule Habit

TODAY . . . **I strengthen my habit to**
RESOLVE CONFLICTS

Last month we shared the idea that every day we have 1,440 minutes to spend for better or for worse. Life today is so filled with frustrations and complex problems, that it would be easy to spend all of those 1,440 minutes being angry about something. This is where all those "rages" come from. Work on yourself to keep from getting caught up in it.

> *You can tell the size of a man*
> *by the size of the thing that makes him mad.*
> ADLAI STEVENSON II

> *Nothing was ever gained by exchanging words in anger.*
> GIL HALSWELL, "TRACKDOWN"

Today: Belittle anger.
In the new millennium, will this "traffic jam" matter?

TODAY . . .   *I strengthen my habit to*
RESOLVE CONFLICTS

The quote below about the hatchet handle, really rings a bell with me.
I'm one of those people who thinks I try to be forgiving. However,
when I read this quote, I realized that when I forgive, I "leave a handle
or two" sticking out for future use. How deeply do you bury the hatch-
ets in your life? Do you see any handles that need to be reburied?

M
A
R

> *Those who say they will forgive but can't forget*
> *– simply bury the hatchet,*
> *but leave the handle out for immediate use.*
> DWIGHT L. MOODY

> *We pardon to the extent that we love.*
> FRANCOIS, DUC DE LA ROCHEFOUCAULD

Today: Bury the hatchet and grind off the handle.

Golden Rule Habit

RESOLVE CONFLICTS in March

25
March
26

TODAY . . .   *I strengthen my habit to*
RESOLVE CONFLICTS

Think of a friend you know well, and then make a list of their faults.
Then review the list to help yourself better understand
why you see these qualities as faults.
Could some of their faults be good attributes in certain circumstances?
How sure are you about their faults?
How important are their faults?
Do they belong in your fault cemetery?

> *We should all keep a large cemetery*
> *in which to bury the faults of friends.*
> ANN LANDERS, ADVICE COLUMNIST

Today: Disagree with dignity – criticize the act, not the person.

74

TODAY . . . **I strengthen my habit to**
RESOLVE CONFLICTS

We have 1,440 minutes every day.
If you were to plan how to use your minutes today, would you plan to use some for fighting, or in anger, or to hate?
How can we be so illogical?
How do we let ourselves be drawn into spending time so illogically?

> *Why hate when you could enjoy your time doing other things?*
> MIRIAM MAKEBA, SOUTH AFRICAN SINGER

> *We must turn to each other and not on each other.*
> REV. JESSE JACKSON

Today: Plan your day well.

27
March
28

RESOLVE CONFLICTS™ in March

𝔊𝔬𝔩𝔡𝔢𝔫 𝔕𝔲𝔩𝔢 Habit

TODAY . . . **I strengthen my habit to**
RESOLVE CONFLICTS

If we could resolve the issue of who is wrong and who is right
in quarrels, there would be very few people fighting.

> *Quarrels would not last long if only one party*
> *were in the wrong.*
> FRANCOIS, DUC DE LA ROCHEFOUCAULD

> *Come over to my side of the argument,*
> *the view is always so clear from here.*
> ASHLEIGH BRILLIANT

Today: Do you care who is wrong and who is right?

TODAY . . .   *I strengthen my habit to*
RESOLVE CONFLICTS

Attitude is a big factor in the resolution of conflict.

Sometimes, we just have to be in an "open-hand" instead of a "clenched fist" frame of mind.

Spend today being open minded and considerate of others.

> *You cannot shake hands*
> *with a clenched fist.*
> INDIRA GANDHI, FORMER PRIME MINISTER OF INDIA

Today: Open your hand – and your heart.

Golden Rule Habit   **29**
                                               March
                                               30

TODAY . . .   *I strengthen my habit to*
RESOLVE CONFLICTS

Of all the quotes I collected for the month of March, this one, by Mark Twain, is one of my favorites. So often our Creator sends us examples through nature. This example of the violet is one to remember. Take this thought with you into April and all through the year.

> *Forgiveness is the fragrance the violet sheds*
> *on the heel that crushed it.*
> MARK TWAIN, AMERICAN AUTHOR AND ESSAYIST

> *Give and forgive.*
> MARIE THERESA RODET GEOGGRIN

Today: Forgive someone – especially you.

TODAY . . .   ***I strengthen my habit to***
                     RESOLVE CONFLICTS

This is it – the 31st of March.
Have you tied up your lions and brought lambs
and white truce flags into your life?
Have you treated yourself to the relief from stress
that resolved conflicts can bring?

You still have 1,440 minutes left
in the month of March to "Resolve Conflicts."
If there is more to do – then do it now.

"Let there be peace on earth and let it begin with me."

31
March

When spider webs unite,
they can tie up a lion.

ETHIOPIAN PROVERB

Silence...
is one of the hardest arguments to refute.

AUTHOR UNKNOWN

If we open a quarrel
        between the past and the present,
we shall find that we have lost
        the future.

SIR WINSTON CHURCHILL

Today: Leave your lions behind and hug a lamb.

CHAPTER 4

take Care
of Our
Environment™

in April and All Year Long!

Color "Cue" - Spring Green

"Together We Can Brighten the World We Share"

IN APRIL, REMEMBER TO...
TAKE CARE OF OUR ENVIRONMENT

It's APRIL – time to refresh and renew our interest in the outdoors. Think green..."Spring Green." Pick a nice day; go outside; take a deep breath and smell the vigorous fresh spring air. Ah–h–h–hhhhhhhh... That big breath of fresh air in our lungs is a good reminder to renew our commitment to the outdoor environment. What we take care of today will be preserved for future generations. This is a time for us to appreciate and enjoy the beauty of the natural world.

> *The supreme reality of our time...*
> *is the vulnerability of this, our planet.*
> JOHN F. KENNEDY, 35TH PRESIDENT OF THE UNITED STATES

It is vital to the future of our community, that we all share a sacred sense of stewardship for our environment. Passing that sense of reverence on to our children this month, is the challenge. Be creative and help them see that we humans are responsible for much of what happens to our world.

We know that our environment is made up of our surroundings; what we see, hear, and breathe. What we often forget is that there is another climate that we live in – the climate of our own relationships. Just for fun, here are a few silly jokes to boost your climate. They are only loosely connected to the environment but – so what.

Q. Where do baby cows eat?   A. In the Cafeteria

Last night I had a dream that I was a tailpipe.   I woke up exhausted.

Have a sunny breezy month. Think spring green. Take care of your environment.

Goal for the Month:

Select a personal, (or family or neighborhood) environmental project and then do something about it. Think about the rest of the world and environmental organizations that would appreciate your financial support.

"Together We Can Brighten the World We All Share"

80

EARTH PLEDGE

MAC GILLIS, GLOBAL EDUCATION ASSOCIATES

I pledge allegiance to the earth,
and all it's sacred parts;
    It's water, land and living things,
    And all it's human hearts.

I pledge allegiance to all life,
And promise I shall care;
    To share and cherish all it's gifts,
    with people everywhere.

Your Name_____

Today's Date_____

TODAY...   *I nourish my habit to*
TAKE CARE OF OUR ENVIRONMENT

Today is April Fool's Day.
Let's hope that we are not fooling ourselves into complacency about the state of our environment. We are the caretakers of the earth for our children and for future generations. Together, let us nourish the habit of earth stewardship this month. There are many quotations that I love. Here is one of them.

> *We have not inherited the earth from our ancestors,*
> *we are borrowing it from our children.*
> AUTHOR UNKNOWN

Remember that you are a very IMPORTANT part of the earth.
Admire and water a flower.

Golden Rule Habit   **1** April   **2**

TODAY...   *I nourish my habit to*
TAKE CARE OF OUR ENVIRONMENT

Let's take a second day to get ourselves in the "stewardship" frame of mind as we nourish our habit this month. More than 35 years ago, John Kennedy recognized that saving our planet would take a global effort, one person at a time. You and I are two people.
We're already on our way.

> *The supreme reality of our time...*
> *is the vulnerability of this, our planet.*
> JOHN F. KENNEDY

Love the earth.
Become the steward of a personal spot somewhere near your home.

TODAY . . .   ***I nourish my habit to***
TAKE CARE OF OUR ENVIRONMENT

Have you ever thought about how we relate to trees as symbols of steadfastness and continuity? We even invented "family trees" to represent family heritage and the future. Think about trees. Imagine yourself deep in a forest glade with the sun filtering down through the leaves.
Do you have a favorite tree somewhere?

A
P
R

He plants trees to benefit another generation.
CAECULIUS STATIUS

Protect our trees.
Look for the recycling emblem on packaging.

3
April

Golden Rule Habit

4

TODAY . . .   ***I nourish my habit to***
TAKE CARE OF OUR ENVIRONMENT

Do justice.

Learn from the world community.

Nurture people.

Cherish nature and the natural order.

Non-conform freely and ethically.

Live responsibly.

Celebrate LIFE.

AUTHOR UNKNOWN

Be pro-active.
Call the chairman of a group and suggest adopting a street.

TODAY... **I nourish my habit to**
TAKE CARE OF OUR ENVIRONMENT

Let's focus today on re-newing our reverence and respect for the beauty of our environment and everything in it – especially for the beauty of one another. Close your eyes and think about the most beautiful place you know. Is it a building or is it a place in nature?

If you truly love nature, you will find beauty everywhere.
VINCENT VAN GOGH

As you go through your day, really SEE what is around you.
Notice a tree, or a small animal or insect.
Notice the delicacy of one simple plant on a co-worker's desk.

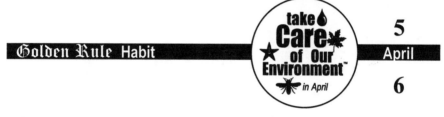

𝕲𝖔𝖑𝖉𝖊𝖓 𝕽𝖚𝖑𝖊 Habit — take Care of Our Environment™ in April — 5 April 6

TODAY... **I nourish my habit to**
TAKE CARE OF OUR ENVIRONMENT

Walt Whitman's poetry emphasizes the dilemma of our human condition, and how uncomfortable sometimes it feels, to be a person instead of a tree. Think like a tree today – firm, tall, knowing yourself, reaching for the heavens and strong against the wind.

I like trees because they seem more comfortable
to the way they have to live than other things do.
WALT WHITMAN, AMERICAN POET

Go on a nature walk. Draw strength from the trees; their power, their tenacity, their steadfast refusal to be bowed down by the winds that rustle their leaves and small branches.

84

TODAY . . . **I nourish my habit to**
                TAKE CARE OF OUR ENVIRONMENT

Appreciate one inch of the ground at your feet.

> *The world cannot be discovered on a journey of miles,*
> *no matter how long,*
> *but only by a spiritual journey of one inch,*
> *very arduous and humbling and joyful,*
> *by which we arrive at the ground beneath our feet,*
> *and learn to beat home.*
> WENDELL BERRY

Watch the journey of one bug for at least five minutes.

7
April

8

Golden Rule Habit

TODAY . . . **I nourish my habit to**
                TAKE CARE OF OUR ENVIRONMENT

Our trees and forests are valuable to the future of our planet.
Oxygen is important to life. Trees breathe in our exhaled
carbon dioxide and breathe out life-giving oxygen.

> *We must take action soon...*
> > *for otherwise no forest – not even in the wildernesses*
> > *of North America – will be safe in the future.*
> > *If we continue this pollution at the present rate,*
> > *there will be scarcely any trees left to worry about*
> > *in a few decades.*
> > JOHN SEYMOUR, BLUEPRINT FOR A GREEN PLANET

Plant a tree.

TODAY . . . ***I nourish my habit to***
TAKE CARE OF OUR ENVIRONMENT

Look for joy in nature today. Whether we notice it or not, joy is abundant in everyday life. Unfortunately, we are often too busy and fail to notice it. Already today, a delicate little hummingbird has come to the feeder outside my window. I will never cease to wonder at the beauty and the energy of that tiny bird. Look for laughter too – laughter has been called a natural tonic for many of life's problems.

The earth laughs in flowers.

RALPH WALDO EMERSON

Today, pick a small bouquet of flowers, or even just one blossom from your yard or an area where no harm would be done.
If this is not possible, then buy just one blossom at a florist and let it "giggle" at you, all day long.

Golden Rule Habit — take Care of Our Environment™ in April — April 9 / 10

TODAY . . . ***I nourish my habit to***
TAKE CARE OF OUR ENVIRONMENT

It may not be too soon to plant seeds or bulbs outside or you can start some inside in a pot or bowl. Some stores have bulb plants like tulips or hyacinths already planted and in bloom for immediate enjoyment. Think deliberately about the beauty of the flowers that will soon greet you. Think about it with anticipation – imagine that it is a gift, on its way to you.

One of the healthiest ways to gamble
is to bet on a spade and a package of garden seeds.

DAN BENNETT

Plant some seeds or bulbs today
– set them on a sunny window ledge and wait.

TODAY . . . **I nourish my habit to**
TAKE CARE OF OUR ENVIRONMENT

The best way to encourage taking care of our environment is to encourage all of us to care more for one another. A genuine concern for others helps us remember the person who may come by next, and might have seen the litter we could have thrown down... but didn't.

> *What the world needs now, is love, sweet love.*
> *That's the only thing that there's too little of.*
> HAL DAVID, AMERICAN COMPOSER

Keep America Beautiful.
Make a list of parks to visit and appreciate soon.

11
April

take **Care** of Our **Environment** *in April*

𝔊𝔬𝔩𝔡𝔢𝔫 ℜ𝔲𝔩𝔢 Habit

12

TODAY . . . **I nourish my habit to**
TAKE CARE OF OUR ENVIRONMENT

Once in a while, it' s a good idea to broaden our perspective by thinking about the big picture. When we feel stuck at home – remember we are always on a free trip around the sun.

> *Only nature does great things for nothing.*
> AUTHOR UNKNOWN

> *Living on earth is expensive but*
> *it includes a free trip around the sun.*
> AUTHOR UNKNOWN

Check out the scenery at no cost to you.
Walk instead of using your car.
Keep the scenery beautiful by putting litter where it belongs.

TODAY... **I nourish my habit to**
TAKE CARE OF OUR ENVIRONMENT

I wonder if Cicero would have written the following quote if he were living down the street from you right now? Drinking in the beauty of flowers and appreciating nature is a need that we DO forget in the rush NOT to forget the things we need from the grocery store like deodorant and sandwich bags.

If you have a garden and a library,
you have everything you need.
CICERO

Fill your need to see beautiful flowers or read beautiful words today. Make your personal environment as uplifting as possible.

Golden Rule Habit — take Care of Our Environment™ in April — 13 April 14

TODAY... **I nourish my habit to**
TAKE CARE OF OUR ENVIRONMENT

Together we all can conserve our water for the years ahead.

We have available for global use, less than 1% of the total earth's supply of water. 97% is in our oceans and 2% is frozen.
DATA FROM: THE WATER POLLUTION CONTROL FEDERATION

How doth the little crocodile improve his shining tail
And pour the waters of the Nile on every golden scale!
LEWIS CARROLL, BRITISH AUTHOR AND POET

Be a water leak detective and a pro-active water conservationist. Shorten your showers, aerate your faucets, put a displacement bag in your toilet tanks, and shorten the water flow when brushing teeth, washing dishes and shaving.

TODAY . . .   *I nourish my habit to*
TAKE CARE OF OUR ENVIRONMENT

There is mounting evidence that having pets lengthens the quality and the duration of life for the sick and the elderly. We all have days when we feel like our pet is the only one who really cares about us. In the old west, there were stories of mountain men like Grizzly Adams, who preferred the company of animals to people.

> *Animals are such agreeable friends*
> *– they ask no questions, they pass no criticisms.*
> GEORGE ELIOT

Give a pet an extra hug or a rub down, or a treat.
If you have an opportunity to help control the pet population, do so.

15
April

16

Golden Rule Habit

TODAY . . .   *I nourish my habit to*
TAKE CARE OF OUR ENVIRONMENT

The Caring Habit color for this month is "Spring Green." Whenever you see green, think of nature and of your responsibility for taking care of the land, the water and the living things around you. Whenever you see green, think, "celebrate nature," in all it's glory. Have you ever been in the middle of a city with only cement all around you? How could we be happy without nature and beautiful living things?

> *Spring is Nature's way of saying, "Let's Party!"*
> ROBIN WILLIAMS

Enjoy the outdoors. Be responsible when you are.
Always cut six-pack rings apart. They aren't biodegradable
and can choke or harm animals and marine life.

TODAY . . .   *I nourish my habit to*
TAKE CARE OF OUR ENVIRONMENT

Nature's perfection is filled with imperfections and no-one seems to mind. As a matter of fact, much of nature's beauty is formed by natural disasters. We can take a lesson from nature when we think we have caused a "disaster" or even when we failed to do our best.

> *The woods would be very silent if no birds sang there except those who sang best.*
>
> JOHN JAMES AUDUBON, NATURALIST

> *A weed is but a modest flower.*
>
> ELLA WHEELER WILCOX - "THE WEED"

If you threw an aluminum can in the trash yesterday
–you can do better today and put one in the re-cycle bin.

Golden Rule Habit

take
Care
★ of Our
Environment™
🐝 *in April*

17
April

18

A
P
R

TODAY . . .   *I nourish my habit to*
TAKE CARE OF OUR ENVIRONMENT

Helen Keller could neither see nor hear.
Here is how she describes the story of her life.
How can we not find joy and beauty in nature?

> *What a joy it is to feel the soft, springy earth*
> *under my feet once more,*
> *to follow grassy roads that lead to ferny brooks*
> *where I can bathe my fingers in a cataract of rippling notes,*
> *or to clamber over a stone wall into green fields*
> *that tumble and roll and climb in riotous gladness!*
>
> HELEN KELLER

Close your eyes and enjoy nature with your other senses –
listen, touch, taste and smell.

90

TODAY ...   *I nourish my habit to*
TAKE CARE OF OUR ENVIRONMENT

Share your growing reverence and sense of stewardship for our environment with children. Watch a nature program on TV with them and talk about what you saw. Discuss with children what they can do to protect our environment and why.

A
P
R

> *The supreme reality of our time...*
> *is the vulnerability of this, our planet.*
> JOHN F. KENNEDY, 35TH UNITED STATES PRESIDENT

Recruit children to learn the "other" 3-R's. Help them nourish their own habits to Reduce, Reuse and Recycle. Encourage them to plant a tree for shade and oxygen.

19
April
20

take ♦
Care
★ of Our
Environment™
in April

Golden Rule Habit

TODAY ...   *I nourish my habit to*
TAKE CARE OF OUR ENVIRONMENT

In America, we honor our Native American people who taught us reverence for the land and for the Great Spirit who made it. Read some Native American poetry or books about the land. An interesting fact about Native American Cherokee hunting traditions is that the warriors always kill the smaller weaker prey. This way, the stronger of each species survives to reproduce.

> *Sell a country! Why not sell the air, the clouds and the great*
> *stream, as well as the earth? Did not the Great Spirit make*
> *them all for the use of His children?*
> TECUMSEH

Share the Cherokee hunting tradition with a hunter you know.

TODAY . . .   I nourish my habit to
TAKE CARE OF OUR ENVIRONMENT

TODAY – think about making an investment in our environment because it is something you value. What do you want to invest in? You can invest in the beauty of your own yard or a neighborhood park. You can make a contribution to an environmental organization or to a specific cause that saves forests or saves an endangered species of animal. Whatever your choice, make an investment today.

The best investment on earth – is earth.
LOUIS GLICKMAN

Help save our Earth.
Send your contribution today.

𝕲olden 𝕽ule Habit

take
Care
of Our
Environment™
in April

21
April
22

TODAY . . .   I nourish my habit to
TAKE CARE OF OUR ENVIRONMENT

This is Earth Day. Celebrate by wearing "Spring Green" and by saying the Earth Pledge. Re-dedicate yourself to doing your part to take care of and nourish our environment.

The Earth Pledge

I pledge allegiance to the earth,
and all it's sacred parts;
It's water, land and living things,
And all it's human hearts.

I pledge allegiance to all life,
And promise I shall care;
To share and cherish all it's gifts,
with people everywhere.

MAC GILLIS, GLOBAL EDUCATION ASSOCIATES

TODAY . . . ***I nourish my habit to***
TAKE CARE OF OUR ENVIRONMENT

Have you considered that the month to take care of our environment is a good time to quit smoking or to encourage someone else to do so? Scientists have proved the dangers of second-hand smoke. What better tribute to nature than to become SMOKE-FREE.

> *The garden of earth is the purest of human pleasures.*
> FRANCIS BACON, BRITISH AUTHOR

A
P
R

Enjoy the human pleasure of nature by giving up the idea that smoking is a pleasure. Become a smoke-free advocate. STOP or begin the process of stopping yourself from smoking. Be an encourager to someone you know, who is trying to become smoke-free.

23
April
24

take
Care
of Our
Environment
in April

Golden Rule Habit

TODAY . . . ***I nourish my habit to***
TAKE CARE OF OUR ENVIRONMENT

People need nourishing too.
WE are part of the environment and we can become withered and starved for affection and attention. Nourish the people around you. Look for ways to praise them.

> *I never saw a wild thing feeling sorry for itself.*
> D.H. LAWRENCE

Nourish people you may not even know. Clean out your closets and basement and give a great load of "stuff" to the Goodwill or the Salvation Army.

TODAY... ***I nourish my habit to***
TAKE CARE OF OUR ENVIRONMENT

April Rain Song
AUTHOR UNKNOWN

Let the rain kiss you.
>*Let the rain beat upon your head*
>*with silver liquid drops.*

Let the rain sing you a lullaby.
>*The rain makes still pools on the sidewalk.*

The rain makes running pools in the gutter.
>*The rain plays a little sleep-song*
>*on our roof at night.*

And I love the rain.

Water is precious – conserve it. Use a broom, not a hose to clean your driveways, paths and steps. Save hundreds of gallons of water. If you really are a conservationist, you can sweep your driveway clean in the rain!

Golden Rule Habit

25
April
26

TODAY... ***I nourish my habit to***
TAKE CARE OF OUR ENVIRONMENT

We learn every day that our earth is fragile
– our atmosphere, our land, our water and our delicate eco-cycle.
Put yourself into nature and renew and refresh a love of the outdoors.
Remember, nature's beauty is free.

>*Grasshoppers are*
>*Chirping in the sleeves*
>*Of a scarecrow.*
>KAWAI CHIGETSU-NI

Go on a nature walk – and breath the fresh air again.
Ah–h–h–hhhhhhhhhhh...
Turn off lights, CDs, TVs & computers when you leave for your walk.

TODAY . . .   *I nourish my habit to*
TAKE CARE OF OUR ENVIRONMENT

Earth Salute

I salute thee, O Earth, bearer of grain,
Bearer of gold, of health, of clothes, of mankind,
Bearer of fruit, of towers, generous, beautiful, unmoving,
Patient, various, fragrant, fertile,
Clad in a cloak all damasked with flowers,
Braided with waters, motley with colors.

        GUILLAUME DE SALLUSTE DU BARTAS

We must all cultivate our earth garden.

        VOLTAIRE, FRENCH AUTHOR

Salute and appreciate the earth
and all of its treasures.

27
April
28

𝔊𝔬𝔩𝔡𝔢𝔫 𝔕𝔲𝔩𝔢 Habit

TODAY . . .   *I nourish my habit to*
TAKE CARE OF OUR ENVIRONMENT

There is nothing lowly in the universe or in our neighborhood
or in our own household. You have 1,440 minutes each day to uplift
and take care of your own family and your own household. This is
where stewardship begins.

Though I have looked everywhere,
I can find nothing lowly in the universe.

        A.R. AMMONS, STILL

What we must decide is how we are valuable
rather than how valuable we are.

        EDGAR Z. FRIEDENBERG

Go to a favorite place in your own home and appreciate what you find
there. Clean it, dust it, sort through stuff – keep what you need and
pass what you don't on to others.

TODAY...   *I nourish my habit to*
TAKE CARE OF OUR ENVIRONMENT

Celebrate every April by planting a tree.
Take note of how much they're growing each spring.

> *He who plants a tree*
> *plants a hope.*
> LUCY LARCOM

> *You can – plant a dream.*
> AUTHOR UNKNOWN

Save other trees by using sponges and cloth
instead of paper towels and napkins.
Use recycled paper at work.

𝔊olden 𝔎ule Habit

take
Care
★ of Our
Environment™
🐝 *in April*

29
April
30

TODAY...   *I nourish my habit to*
TAKE CARE OF OUR ENVIRONMENT

This is the last day of April. You have faithfully worked on nourishing
your habit to take care of our environment. Remember that every day,
the earth calls us directly. If we listen, we will allow her to keep on
reminding us of her needs.

She speaks boisterously with blazing flower hues and arrogantly
with the dash of rustling willows. She glows in the bright green of a
new spring leaf, and caresses us with the feel of a water-worn stone.
She embraces us with the fresh smell of a summer rain, and touches
our hearts through the brush of the evening breeze on our skin.
AUTHOR UNKNOWN

Have a sunny, breezy day. As you leave the month of April, reflect on
how well you have acquired the habit of stewardship for our environment. Thank you for all that you do and will do in the years ahead.

CHAPTER 5

Be
Appreciative™

*in **May** and All Year Long!*

Color "Cue" - Grateful Pink

"Together We Can Brighten the World We All Share."

Give a gift of the *Golden Rule Revolution* to the people in your life.
For quantity pricing see the card at the back of this book. If someone else has used this form, you may
phone: 724-453-0447 e.mail: allofus@icubed.com or visit our website: www.goldenrulerevolution.com

---

IN MAY, REMEMBER TO...
BE APPRECIATIVE

Since I know about the GOLDEN RULE REVOLUTION, I already celebrate "Be Appreciative" in May. When I see pink, I see "Grateful Pink" and think of someone I want to appreciate.

I traditionally send many thank you notes. It has already become a "tradition" for me to do this. Perhaps, by joining the GOLDEN RULE REVOLUTION, you will begin the "Be Appreciate in May" tradition along with me. I know I have thirty one days to work on being more grateful and appreciative. I have thirty-one days to catch up on sending thank you notes to people that I meant to send to... and didn't... or to people I just want to remember as being special in my life. I think the people who receive my notes are surprised and pleased. I know that I feel a deep sense of warmth down inside when my handful of thank you envelopes goes into the postal slot.

You know, there is a lot to the theory that happiness is derived more from your own state of mind, than from anything else. It's sort of like the old Peace Corps test of whether you are an optimist or a pessimist. They show you a picture of a glass half filled with liquid and ask you to describe it. It's the same picture and the same glass. The only difference is the perspective of the viewer who looks at it. An optimist will see the glass as half full. A pessimist will see it as half empty.

Gratitude and appreciation are like that. When you are filled with gratitude and appreciation, then you can't be filled with longing, or greed, or envy, or jealousy. You don't need to read a two hundred and fifty page book to learn that you don't feel happy, when you are feeling envious.

In the last several years, Oprah Winfrey has become involved in the "kindness movement" and in helping her viewers find health and happiness in their own lives. She suggests that one of the best ways to change your own perspective and attitude is to keep a "Grateful Journal." The Grateful Journal is a notebook you keep near your bedside.

Every night before going to sleep, she suggests that you write down in the Journal, at least five things that you are grateful for that day. I have been doing that for a while – not perfectly – but enough to know it works. It keeps my mind focused on the positive moments of each day instead of moments that might have brought me down.

We all know that kind caring attitudes and behavior create a win/win for us and others. Caring attitudes fulfill the standard set by the words of the Golden Rule, "Do to others what you would like done to you." Take time this month to celebrate "Be Appreciative" in your own life and in your own way. Notice and appreciate workers you pass by on the street or talk to as you move through your day. Notice that person washing windows over there. How about telling them how nice the windows look as you pass by. Tell your children why you appreciate them. And don't forget to appreciate yourself. You are important too.

Goal for the Month:

> In addition to appreciating others, take time to appreciate yourself — do something you've always wanted to do!

> *"Together We Can Brighten the World We All Share."*

APPRECIATING MOTHER

MULTIPLE UNKNOWN AUTHORS VIA THE INTERNET

My Mother taught me LOGIC...
*"If you fall off that swing and break your neck,
you can't go to the store with me."*

My Mother taught me MEDICINE...
"If you keep crossing your eyes, they're going to freeze that way."

My Mother taught me TO THINK AHEAD...
"If you don't pass your spelling test, you'll never get a good job!"

My Mother taught me ESP...
*"Put your sweater on;
don't you think that I know when you're cold?"*

My Mother taught me TO MEET A CHALLENGE...
*"What were you thinking? Answer me when I talk to you.
Don't talk back to me!"*

My Mother taught me HUMOR...
*"When that lawn mower cuts off your toes,
don't come running to me."*

My Mother taught me how to BECOME AN ADULT...
"If you don't eat your vegetables, you'll never grow up."

My mother taught me ABOUT SEX...
"How do you think you got here?"

My mother taught me about GENETICS...
"You are just like your father!"

My mother taught me about my ROOTS...
"Do you think you were born in a barn?"

My mother taught me about the WISDOM of AGE...
"When you get to be my age, you will understand."

My mother taught me about ANTICIPATION...
"Just wait until your father gets home."

My mother taught me about RECEIVING...
"You are going to get it when we get home."

And my all-time favorite thing – JUSTICE...
*"One day you will have kids, and I hope they turn out just like
YOU... then you'll see what it's like!"*

★ ★ ★

Our Flag
AUTHOR UNKNOWN

It's Red for Love,
and it's White for Law
And it's Blue for the Hope
that Our Forefathers saw.

★ ★ ★

TODAY... **I cherish my habit to
BE APPRECIATIVE**

Today is May Day. This has become the traditional day to celebrate the coming of spring. In medieval England, May Day's main event was the Maypole Dance. Colorful dancers holding ribbons danced around the pole to welcome spring. Appreciating the beauty of nature is a great note to start off May – the month to "Be Appreciative."

> *Gratitude is the sign of noble souls.*
> AESOP, GREEK AUTHOR

This month, practicing praise and appreciation for others will help develop your own "attitude of gratitude." At the bottom of this month's Daily Habit Inspirations, you'll find a "Praise" phrase to practice as many times as you can during that day.

Praise Phrase # 1 – "You're great."

Golden Rule Habit **1 May**

2

TODAY... **I cherish my habit to
BE APPRECIATIVE**

Life isn't perfect.

So often I catch myself falling into a state of feeling bad about what isn't the way I want it to be.

Thank you Helen Keller for these words...

> *I thank God for my handicaps, for through them,
> I have found myself,
> my work, and my God.*
> HELEN KELLER, AMERICAN AUTHOR (BLIND)

Praise Phrase # 2 – "You're very special."

TODAY . . . **I cherish my habit to**
BE APPRECIATIVE

Keeping ourselves in a grateful frame of mind is a great way to have a good day. Oprah Winfrey has found a way to increase our "attitude of gratitude" – the "Grateful Journal." This is a notebook (any notebook will do) that you keep near your bedside. Every night, she suggests that you write down in the Journal, at least five things that you are grateful for that day.

Start a Grateful Journal and keep it going all month long.

> *Gratitude is the memory of the heart.*
> J.B. MASSIEU

Praise Phrase # 3 – "Thank You."

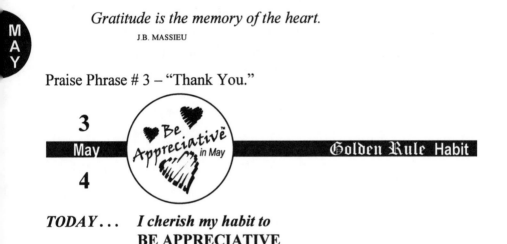

TODAY . . . **I cherish my habit to**
BE APPRECIATIVE

While we're encouraging ourselves to praise and appreciate more,
it's a good idea to think about the other end of the equation,
– being the recipient of praise.

> *Praise, if you don't swallow it, can't hurt you.*
> MORT WALKER, CREATOR, "BEETLE BAILEY" COMIC STRIP

> *Praise can be your most valuable weapon*
> *as long as you don't aim at yourself.*
> O.A. BATTISTA

Praise Phrase # 4 – "I appreciate your humble attitude."

TODAY...   *I cherish my habit to*
BE APPRECIATIVE

During May, let's take time to show appreciation wherever we can.
Make that pot of coffee for a busy spouse.
Hug your child.
Or clean the kitchen.
Or wipe the blackboard.
Or put paper in the copier at work.

> *He who received a benefit should never forget it;*
> *he who bestows one should never remember it.*
> CHARRON

P.S. And if, for a few minutes, there's no one around to appreciate, give a little to the sun, to the air and to a tree!
Praise Phrase # 5 – "You make a difference."

Golden Rule Habit   *Be Appreciative in May*   **5**   **May**   **6**

TODAY...   *I cherish my habit to*
BE APPRECIATIVE

We were taught to say "thank you" because it was "good manners."
What I've learned since then, is that "thankfulness" is so much more than just good manners. Thankfulness is a way of life. It is the path to fulfillment and a life full of joy.

> *A thankful heart is not only the greatest virtue,*
> *but the parent of all other virtues.*
> CICERO

> *Thankfulness is a sure index of spiritual health.*
> MAURICE DAMETZ

Practice Praise Phrase # 6 – "I am thankful for you."

TODAY . . .   I cherish my habit to
BE APPRECIATIVE

Mother's Day is just around the corner. Mothers are real people in our own lives. The concept of mothering symbolizes the quality of cherishment for all living things – hence "mother nature." Mom's aren't perfect – but they are yours. This month take time to do more for your mom than send a card or call. Start with the question, "What would mom most like from me today?"

> *You only have one mom and you should appreciate her.*
> SAM, AGE 12

> *A company held a contest for kids with the theme:*
> *"The Nicest Thing My Father Ever Did For Me."*
> *One answer: "He married my mother."*
> ROBERT SYLVESTER

Praise Phrase # 7 –
"Thanks mom, you're the best."

7
May

8

𝕲𝖔𝖑𝖉𝖊𝖓 𝕽𝖚𝖑𝖊 Habit

TODAY . . .   I cherish my habit to
BE APPRECIATIVE

If all of my good intentions were laid end to end... oh what a long road they would pave. I opened a drawer this morning and found an addressed thank you note that I had forgotten to send. What makes this month great is that we can use it to play "appreciation catch-up." It's never too late to say thank you.

> *The smallest good act is better*
> *than the most magnificent promises.*
> MACAULAY

> *A great way to say "THANKS" is to*
> *"PASS IT ON" when we can't return a favor.*
> JEFFEREY A. PATRICK

Praise Phrase # 8 – "Thanks for showing me you care."

TODAY...   *I cherish my habit to*
BE APPRECIATIVE

Years ago, when my son went through a "negative attitude" phase we gave him *The Praise Book*. The point was that there is always something good you can say about everyone such as *"You have great elbows,"* or *"What a neat cupboard,"* or *"You always have a nice smile."* Try writing your own praise book this month with the things you say and do for others.

> *When someone does something good, applaud!*
> *You will make two people happy.*
> SAMUEL GOLDWYN, AMERICAN FILM MAKER

> *Find the good and praise it.*
> ALEX HALEY, AMERICAN AUTHOR

Praise Phrase # 9 – "Hooray for you."

Golden Rule Habit   *Be Appreciative in May*   **9 May 10**

TODAY...   *I cherish my habit to*
BE APPRECIATIVE

Count your blessings is a phrase everyone knows – but it is easy to forget when our favorite shirt comes out of the dryer shrunken down two sizes.

> *Blessings brighten while we count them.*
> MALTHIE D. BABCOCK

> *Better to lose count while naming your blessings*
> *than to lose your blessings by counting your troubles.*
> MALTHIE D. BABCOCK

Praise Phrase # 10 – "I appreciate your work."
> *(Be cautious if you're saying this to*
> *the person who shrunk your shirt.)*

TODAY . . . **I cherish my habit to
BE APPRECIATIVE**

Sometimes it does us good to appreciate the natural gifts that
surround us – the air, the trees, flowers and the sunshine or the rain.
Sit quietly on a bench in the park or on a rock in the forest
and look around you. Notice the gifts.

> *God took the time to create beauty,
> how can we be too busy to appreciate it?*
> RANDALL B. CORBIN

**M
A
Y**

Praise Phrase # 11 – "You put a smile on my face."

11
May

12

TODAY . . . **I cherish my habit to
BE APPRECIATIVE**

Mary Poppins said, *"A spoonful of sugar makes the medicine go down."*
There's also an old adage, *"You catch more flies with honey than with
vinegar."* Ben Franklin was credited with the quote,
"Diplomacy is the art of helping someone else to have your idea."
Giving respect and appreciation creates a two way street that business
people call the "win/win" way.

> *Use soft words and hard arguments.*
> ENGLISH PROVERB

Praise Phrase # 12 – "You've got it now."

TODAY . . .   *I cherish my habit to*
BE APPRECIATIVE

One of the most difficult aspects of appreciation is expecting it.
We know that we "shouldn't" expect anything in return
when we give to others – but doing it is easier said than done.
Building our habit of giving without expecting gratitude,
is a good attribute to work on this month.

> *Gratitude is a sometime thing in this world.*
> *Just because you've been feeding them all winter,*
> *don't expect the birds to take it easy on your grass seed.*
> BILL VAUGHAN

Praise Phrase # 13 – "You've earned a big hug for doing good
without expecting gratitude."

Golden Rule Habit   Be Appreciative in May   **13 May 14**

TODAY . . .   *I cherish my habit to*
BE APPRECIATIVE

Many things are done behind people's back that are harmful. Gossip is one of the worst in my book. Quiet gratitude, in the form of a real "pat on the back," is one of the best ideas I've heard. Increasing your gratitude and praise vocabulary this month will bring benefits all year long.

> *The best thing to do behind a person's back is to pat it.*
> FRANKLIN P. JONES

> *Words of praise can heal relationships, resolve conflicts*
> *and improve your chances of professional success.*
> WILLIAM F. O'DELL

Praise Phrase # 14 – "I appreciate your directness."

TODAY . . .   ***I cherish my habit to***
                       BE APPRECIATIVE

Manners are important. We can rely on manners to help us get through some tense moments once in a while. However, when manners come from the heart as well as from Amy Vanderbuilt's Etiquette books, there is more caring and joy in the moment for all.

> *Gratitude is when memory is stored*
> *in the heart and not in the mind.*
> SAM N. HAMPTON

> *The manner in which it is given*
> *is worth more than the gift.*
> PIERRE CORNEILLE

Praise Phrase # 15 –
"I appreciate your friendship."

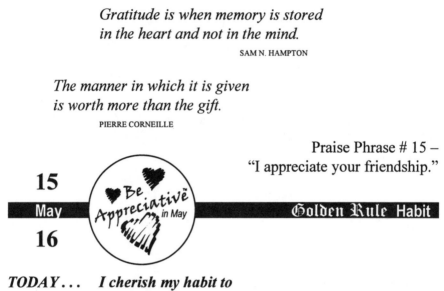

15
May   𝕲𝖔𝖑𝖉𝖊𝖓 𝕽𝖚𝖑𝖊 Habit
16

TODAY . . .   ***I cherish my habit to***
                       BE APPRECIATIVE

The "ILYAITYT" bedtime tradition began in our home more than 30 years ago. Today it is still our special shorthand for the kind of love children need and want. You can start the ILYAITYT tradition in your household this month. Make this secret code the last thought you share with your children just before they fall asleep every night. Oh yes, you'll need to know what it means. ILYAITYT stands for "I LOVE YOU AND I THINK YOU'RE TERRIFIC!"

> *If you want your children to improve, let them hear*
> *the nice things you say about them to others.*
> HAIM GINOTT, PSYCHOLOGIST

Praise Phrase # 16 – "ILYAITYT."

TODAY... ***I cherish my habit to***
BE APPRECIATIVE

I often wonder why business books and books about how to get along with people are on different shelves at the store. Andrew Carnegie said that business success is 89% people skills and only 11% technical skills.

I have yet to find the man, however exalted his station,
who did not do better work and put forth the greater effort
under a spirit of approval than under a spirit of criticism.
CHARLES SCHWAB, AMERICAN FINANCIER

Sandwich every piece of criticism between two layers of praise.
MARY KAY ASH, FOUNDER, MARY KAY COSMETICS

People ask you for criticism, but they only want praise.
W. SOMERSET MAUGHAM, BRITISH AUTHOR, OF HUMAN BONDAGE

Praise Phrase # 17 – "Good job."

Golden Rule Habit

17
May
18

TODAY... ***I cherish my habit to***
BE APPRECIATIVE

Here are two quotes that together – say a volume of truths.

At the deepest place in human nature
is the craving to be appreciated.
WILLIAM JAMES

No one notices what I do until I don't do it.
LORRIE, AGE 14

Praise Phrase # 18 – "You mean the world to me."

112

TODAY . . .   I cherish my habit to
BE APPRECIATIVE

It's so great when once in a while we encounter
kind surprises from strangers we will never see again.
The "random acts of kindness" movement encourages this.
When we can't repay a kindness, or even when we can,
the best way to "Be Appreciative" is to pass it on.

> *Have you had a kindness shown?*
> *Pass it on.*
> HENRY BURTON, "PASS IT ON"

M
A
Y

Praise Phrase # 19 – "Thanks for caring."

19
May
20

𝕲𝖔𝖑𝖉𝖊𝖓 𝕽𝖚𝖑𝖊 Habit

TODAY . . .   I cherish my habit to
BE APPRECIATIVE

I have read sad stories in books like *Chicken Soup* about people who
failed to appreciate their loved ones and to praise them before losing
them. You can write your own "happy ending" stories by remembering to be appreciative on a regular basis.

> *Please teach me to appreciate what I have*
> *before time forces me to appreciate what I had.*
> SUSAN L. LENZKES

> *Look at everything as though you were seeing it either for the first*
> *or last time. Then your time on earth will be filled with glory.*
> BETTY SMITH, A TREE GROWS IN BROOKLYN

Praise Phrase # 20 – "I'm so glad you're in my life."

TODAY... *I cherish my habit to*
BE APPRECIATIVE

Everyone has great blessings in their lives.
No one is an exception.

Be appreciative.

It is not what we say about our blessings
but how we use them
that is the true measure of our thanksgiving.
W.T. PURKISER

Praise Phrase # 21 – "You can do it, you're on your way."

Golden Rule Habit   Be Appreciative in May   **21 May 22**

TODAY... *I cherish my habit to*
BE APPRECIATIVE

Because we have so many of them, it greatly improves our outlook to appreciate and be grateful for the treasures of normal days. Did you notice the beautiful child with her mother that you passed on the street today, or the shape of a cloud in the sky?

Normal day, let me be aware of the treasure you are.
MARY JEAN IRION

He who receives a benefit with gratitude
repays the first installment on his debt.
SENECA INDIAN SAYING

Praise Phrase # 22 – "You're special."

114

TODAY . . . ***I cherish my habit to***
BE APPRECIATIVE

An anonymous quote I've heard many times is, "I never saw a U-Haul Truck in a funeral procession." It's humorous but true – we don't really own anything but our hearts and our spirit. Even our bodies are rented for a certain length of time. From this "bottom line" perspective, think about "being appreciative."

> *I don't have to have millions of dollars to be happy.*
> *All I need is to have some clothes on my back, eat a decent meal*
> *when I want to, and get a little loving when I feel like it.*
> *That's the bottom line, man.*
>
> RAY CHARLES, AMERICAN SINGER

Praise Phrase # 23 – "I'm impressed."

23
May
24

𝔊𝔬𝔩𝔡𝔢𝔫 𝔕𝔲𝔩𝔢 Habit

TODAY . . . ***I cherish my habit to***
BE APPRECIATIVE

Legacy of the Teacher
JACK PRELUTSKY

> *I leave you love.*
>   *I leave you hope.*
> *I leave you the challenge*
>   *of developing confidence in one another.*
>
> *I leave you a thirst for education.*
>   *I leave you respect for the use of power.*
> *I leave you faith.*
>   *I leave you the dignity of your heritage and your future.*

Praise Phrase # 24 – "I've got faith in you."

TODAY . . .   I cherish my habit to
BE APPRECIATIVE

Teacher Appreciation Week is in May. No matter what age we are, it's time to appreciate those special teachers in our lives. Remembering our teachers is a must. Quietly, in your mind and heart, remember and appreciate one special teacher. If you can reach them, let them know.

The class in school I hate the most is the one I learn the most from.
JOANNE, AGE 10

Teachers are the best people in the whole world.
NATKA, AGE 14

Sometimes a teacher who seems to be totally boring
at the beginning of the year, turns out to be the most awesome!
ROBERT, AGE 12

Praise Phrase # 25 –
"You're my teacher and my friend."

Golden Rule Habit

Be Appreciative™ in May

25
May
26

TODAY . . .   I cherish my habit to
BE APPRECIATIVE

There is so much publicity about the problems kids have today and parents are being blamed for most of it. Let's start a rally this month, to appreciate parents more and to criticize them less. After all, the best way to inspire anyone to improve is with praise and encouragement. Parents are no exception.

Parents don't get enough appreciation. If you want to make your
parents feel good, write them a small note that says, "I love you."
KIM, AGE 11

Thanks an awful lot, Dad.
It sure is good when your father's a friend.
BEAVER CLEAVER, "LEAVE IT TO BEAVER"

Praise Phrase # 26 – "I love you mom and dad."

TODAY . . .   ***I cherish my habit to***
                 BE APPRECIATIVE

Appreciate yourself today.
This one is for you.
Have a month filled with joy and gratitude.
Thank you for joining the GOLDEN RULE REVOLUTION
and for all you do.

> *Make the kind of memories that you want to live with forever.*
> **AUTHOR UNKNOWN**

> *Were there no God, we would be in this glorious world*
> *with grateful hearts and no one to thank.*
> **CHRISTINA ROSSETTI**

Praise Phrase # 27 –
"What would I ever do without you."

27
May

28

𝕲𝖔𝖑𝖉𝖊𝖓 𝕽𝖚𝖑𝖊 𝕳𝖆𝖇𝖎𝖙

TODAY . . .   ***I cherish my habit to***
                 BE APPRECIATIVE

In May, we celebrate Memorial Day.
It is a weekend of fun and picnics and enjoying the company of family
and friends. During this weekend, we should remember to quietly honor
and praise those who served and those who died, for the principles of
the United States of America.

> *It is less appropriate*
> *to mourn the loss of valiant men who died*
> *than to thank God that such men lived.*
> **GEORGE S. PATTON, UNITED STATES GENERAL, WORLD WAR II**

Praise Phrase # 28 – "I honor YOU."

TODAY... ***I cherish my habit to***
BE APPRECIATIVE

Cultivating a garden, or cultivating a kindness are both works of beauty. Appreciate them both.

> *Kind hearts are the garden,*
>
> *Kind thoughts are the roots,*
>
> *Kind words are the blossoms,*
>
> *Kind deeds are the fruit.*
>
> JOHN RUSKIN

Praise Phrase # 29 – "Thank you for your kindness."

🙟𝔬𝔩𝔡𝔢𝔫 𝔯𝔲𝔩𝔢 Habit   Be Appreciative™ in May   **29** May **30**

TODAY... ***I cherish my habit to***
BE APPRECIATIVE

If there is a universal language of appreciation, it is a smile. Try yours out in the mirror this morning. I'll bet you haven't seen it yourself for a while. Now try it out on everyone you meet today – they all try hard with their own lives and deserve appreciation too.

> *In all the countries I've been to,*
> *everyone understands and appreciates a smile.*
> JENNIFER, AGE 14

> *Those who can receive bread and smile in gratitude*
> *can feed many without even realizing it.*
> HENRI J. M. NOUWEN

Praise Phrase # 30 – "What a great smile, you brighten my day."

118

TODAY . . . **I cherish my habit to**
BE APPRECIATIVE

It's the end of May. I appreciate you. I appreciate that you have this book in your hand right now and are reading this. It means that we share a deep desire to make our own lives and the lives of those around us better. We can make a habit out of appreciating the fragile thread of life and treasuring the joy life brings.

We can be thankful for what we have or complain about what we do not have. One or the other becomes the habit pattern of our own life.
ELISABETH ELLIOTT

Gratitude is the most exquisite form of courtesy.
JACQUES MARITAIN

Praise Phrase # 31 – "I appreciate you, the reader of this page."

31
May

Golden Rule Habit
MAY POSTSCRIPT

In MAY and All Year Long...

I cherish my habit to
BE APPRECIATIVE.

CHAPTER 6

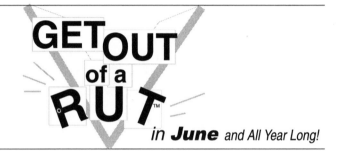

Color "Cue" - JOLT! Orange

"Together We Can Brighten the World We All Share."

IN JUNE, REMEMBER TO...
GET OUT OF A RUT

I will Dream; I will Be Adventurous; I will Improve Myself.

This month's celebration color is "JOLT Orange." The color orange never gets lost in a rut or a crowd and cries out to be different. Use orange as your secret reminder to dream...and to go for accomplishing the goals you want to reach. Encourage yourself to have faith and confidence – know that you CAN do it – whatever it is.

Feel the Daily Inspirations uplift you and set you free from the boundaries around you. Feel uplifted in your heart toward your own dreams. Of all the twelve habits – this month "Get Out of Your Rut," is more enjoyably achieved when it is inspired. We are able to bloom and grow in direct ratio to our willingness to dream.

> *Whatever You can do or Dream you can, Begin It.*
> *BOLDNESS has Genius, Power and Magic in it.*
> JOHANN GOETHE

Needless to say, I have read thousands of quotes while I have been working on the GOLDEN RULE REVOLUTION to help each of us become our "better selves" more often. So many of them have reflected on the beauty of an inspired life. Here is a quote to start off June. It is a favorite because it makes me laugh and cry at the same time.

> *Millions long for immortality who don't know*
> *what to do on a rainy afternoon.*
> SUSAN ERTZ

Goal for the Month:

> Break free of procrastination. Begin something
> that you have been putting off for too long.

"Together We Can Brighten the World We All Share"

"Whatever you can do... or dream you can—Begin it.
BOLDNESS has genius, power and magic in it."

JOHANN W. GOETHE

Until one is committed there is hesitancy;
the chance to draw back;
always ineffectiveness.

Concerning all acts of initiative and creations,
there is one elementary truth,
the ignorance of which kills countless ideas
and splendid plans.

That the moment one definitely commits oneself,
providence moves too.

All sorts of things occur to help one
that would never have otherwise occurred.

A whole stream of events issues from the decision,
raising in one's favor,
all manner of unforeseen incidents and meetings
and material assistance which no (wo)man
could have dreamt would have come their way.

W.H. MURRAY

TODAY ...   *I discover my habit to*
GET OUT OF A RUT!

Take an extra moment to re-inspire your daily journey through June by re-reading and reflecting on the three poems at the beginning of the chapter. Read them every day. Feel your heart uplifted and guided toward your dreams. Of all the twelve Golden Rule Habits – "Get Out of A Rut" is nourished by faith, courage and inspiration. Growth only happens when there are dreams guiding your journey of joy.

> *Growth is the only evidence of life.*
> JOHN HENRY CARDINAL NEWMAN, BRITISH THEOLOGIAN

> *On this narrow planet, we have only the choice between two unknown worlds.*
> COLETTE, FRENCH AUTHOR

Choose new life, confidence,
love, joy, faith, hope.

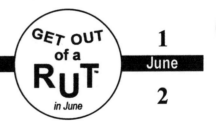

Golden Rule Habit   GET OUT of a RUT in June   1 June 2

J U N

TODAY ...   *I discover my habit to*
GET OUT OF A RUT!

Nobody ever said life is easy. So often, we postpone our dreams until "things smooth out" or until our problems disappear, or until we have more time. Dreams will never happen in our lives unless we start toward them now. Tough times are often the most fertile ground for converting problems into opportunities we never believed would come our way.

> *When the going gets tough, the tough get going.*
> JOSEPH P. KENNEDY, FATHER OF PRESIDENT JOHN F. KENNEDY

> *If there is no struggle there is no progress.*
> FREDERICK DOUGLAS

Wear orange, or an orange accessory – notice orange today.

TODAY... **I discover my habit to**
GET OUT OF A RUT!

A "dream" happens all in one night, but our living hopes and dreams never materialize that fast. Whatever your self-improvement goals are this month – they will happen in a series of many small steps – some firm, some faltering, and some altogether wrong that must be re-directed. I call this series of steps toward dreams, "the bread crumb path." What will you call the path you walk?

> *According to the ancient Chinese proverb,*
> *A journey of a thousand miles must begin with a single step.*
> JOHN F. KENNEDY, 35TH PRESIDENT OF THE UNITED STATES

> *Mountain, get out of my way.*
> MONTEL WILLIAMS, TALK-SHOW HOST

Eat just one potato chip, then put the bag away.

3
June
4

GET OUT of a RUT in June

𝕲𝖔𝖑𝖉𝖊𝖓 𝕽𝖚𝖑𝖊 Habit

JUN

TODAY... **I discover my habit to**
GET OUT OF A RUT!

It's so easy to keep life just the way it is. Is this your daily schedule?

6:00 am	*Alarm rings*
6:15 am	*Alarm rings again*
6:30 am	*Hit the shower*
7:00 am	*Feed kids and get them off to school*
8:00 am	*Leave for work*
9:00 - 12:00 pm	*WORK*
12:00 - 1:00 pm	*Lunch*
1:00 - 5:00 pm	*WORK*
6:00 pm	*Dinner*
8:00 pm - ?	*Put kids to bed*
10:00 pm - ?	*Fall asleep while watching TV*

Tuck a special little note, into a lunch bag, briefcase, pocket or purse.

TODAY . . . *I discover my habit to*
GET OUT OF A RUT!

Make at least one difficult decision today.

> *Just because you have 4 chairs, 6 plates, and 3 cups,*
> *is no reason why you can't invite 12 people to dinner.*
> ALICE MAY BROCK, AMERICAN RESTAURANTEUR

> *The difficulty in life is the choice.*
> GEORGE MOORE, "THE BENDING OF THE BOUGH"

> *We cannot become what we need to be by remaining what we are.*
> MAX DE PERE, LEADERSHIP IS AN ART

Draw a map of your journey.
Mark the difficult decision points with an erasable pen.

Golden Rule Habit — GET OUT of a RUT™ *in June* — June 5 6

J U N

TODAY . . . *I discover my habit to*
GET OUT OF A RUT!

Most choices involve going "towards" or "away" from something or someone. Think about your choices today – what "loss" are you risking by taking a step toward your goals. Is there fear? Is the fear and the risk of loss holding you back? What is your "second base"? Take one step to get there.

> *Progress always involves risk;*
> *you can't steal second base and keep your foot on first.*
> FREDERICK WILCOX

> *I don't want the cheese, I just want to get out of the trap.*
> SPANISH PROVERB

> *Why not go out on a limb? Isn't that where the fruit is?*
> FRANK SCULLY

Find a tree and climb it. Look at life from a higher perspective.

126

TODAY... *I discover my habit to*
GET OUT OF A RUT!

Have you ever contemplated how impossible human flight must have seemed before the "first flight" on December 17, 1903?
How impossible did flight seem to Wilber and Orville Wright?
What do you believe is impossible in your life?
Write an action plan and timetable to accomplish your "Impossible."

I have learned to use the word impossible with the greatest caution.
WERNHER VON BRAUN, GERMAN ROCKET SCIENTIST

Determine that the thing can and shall be done,
and then we shall find the way.
ABRAHAM LINCOLN, 16TH PRESIDENT OF THE UNITED STATES

Watch and wait for the first star to appear in the evening sky.
It is your star.

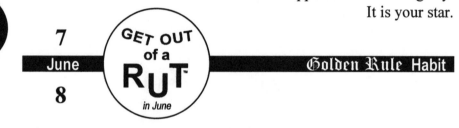

JUN

7
June
8

GET OUT of a RUT in June

𝔊𝔬𝔩𝔡𝔢𝔫 𝔯𝔲𝔩𝔢 Habit

TODAY... *I discover my habit to*
GET OUT OF A RUT!

The first step is the hardest. The first step contains a fear of the unknown that we only have to overcome once – to move ahead. It seems simple enough – but we know it is not. Think about the time you took the first step to resolve an argument. Do you remember the fear? After the argument was resolved, do you remember the joy and the relief of regaining a friendship that was once lost?

You miss 100% of the shots you never take. WAYNE GRETZKY

It takes guts to leave the ruts. ELAINE PARKE

Either move or be moved! COLIN POWELL, RETIRED UNITED STATES GENERAL

Forgive someone whom you thought you couldn't – do it today.

TODAY...   *I discover my habit to*
GET OUT OF A RUT!

Because you are reading this book, you are not one of America's illiterate adults. Let the courage of those who have entered literacy programs and learned to read, inspire you to read more often. Read to a child whenever you can. Remember, you are one of the lucky ones.

> *To delight in reading is to trade life's dreamy moments*
> *for moments of pure joy.*
> CHARLES DE SECONDAT, BARON DE MONTESQUIEU

> *Books are keys to wisdom's treasure;*
> *Books are gates to lands of pleasure;*
> *Books are paths that upward lead;*
> *Books are friends. Come, let us read.*
> EMILIE POULSSON

Volunteer in an adult literacy program
or read to a child.

GET OUT of a RUT in June

9

Golden Rule Habit   **June**

10

J U N

TODAY...   *I discover my habit to*
GET OUT OF A RUT!

Boldness doesn't have to be loud and pushy. Boldness is the quiet first step of courage...the step that is most difficult to take. The quote below is by the German poet, Johann W. Goethe. It is one of my all time favorites. His words inspired me to leave my "cushy" jobs in corporate America to bring to life my dream – that these caring habits of the Golden Rule can encourage us all toward a better life.

> *Whatever you can do or dream you can begin it.*
> *Boldness has genius, power and magic in it.*
> JOHANN W. GOETHE

Sit outside in nature and dream –
Who are you?...What are your gifts?...What is your calling?...

TODAY...   ***I discover my habit to***
GET OUT OF A RUT!

Thomas Edison tried nearly 1,000 ways to make a light bulb
before he found the one way that worked. Thankfully,
he did NOT have an instruction book! He knew that
discoveries are partly inspiration and mostly perspiration.

*Discoveries are often made by not following instructions;
by going off the main road; by trying the untried.*
FRANK TYGER

Trials are trails to higher ground.
S. SAMUEL VENECHANOS

Find a nearby park with walking trails.
Choose to follow a path you have never taken before.

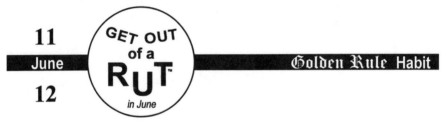

11
June
12

GET OUT
of a
R U T
in June

𝕲𝖔𝖑𝖉𝖊𝖓 𝕽𝖚𝖑𝖊 Habit

J U N

TODAY...   ***I discover my habit to***
GET OUT OF A RUT!

Vision and wonder go hand in hand. There is a "sacred" quality to
wonder. Life is sweet when we remain childlike with a capacity for
wonder and awe. Too often we think that "being a grown-up" means
leaving "wonder" behind.

Life is the childhood of our immortality.
JOHANN GOETHE

*The world will never starve for wonders,
but only for want of wonder.*
G.K. CHESTERTON, BRITISH AUTHOR

Vision is the art of seeing things invisible.
JONATHAN SWIFT, BRITISH AUTHOR

Observe with wonder— a flower...an insect...a bird...a child.

TODAY . . . **I discover my habit to**
GET OUT OF A RUT!

Curiosity is a first cousin to wonder and vision. I think curiosity is the spice of life. What fun it is to make a discovery, even a small one. What discovery did you make yesterday. Perhaps you discovered many new things.

> *Be curious always! For knowledge will not acquire you;*
> *you must acquire it.*
> SUDIE BACK

> *Nothing is interesting if you're not interested.*
> HELEN MACINNESS

Decide to learn something new. Look it up in an encyclopedia or find it on the internet. Perhaps learning to use the internet is the challenge you want to conquer this month.

Golden Rule Habit

GET OUT of a **RUT** in June

13

June

14

J U N

TODAY . . . **I discover my habit to**
GET OUT OF A RUT!

Today is Flag Day.
On this day in 1777, Americans adopted our flag.

> *In America,*
> *getting on in the world means*
> *getting out of the world we have known before.*
> ELLERY SEDGWICK, THE HAPPY PROFESSION

> *In America,*
> *nobody says you have to keep the circumstances*
> *somebody else created for you.*
> AMY TAN, JAPANESE-AMERICAN AUTHOR, THE JOY LUCK CLUB

What does America mean to you?
If you don't have a flag, buy one and hang it today.

130

TODAY...   *I discover my habit to*
          GET OUT OF A RUT!

It's halfway through June.
Here are some quick and easy-to-do ideas for "getting out of a rut."
>*Read a book to your child*
>*Ride a bike trail.*
>*Visit a historical site.*
>*Learn to play a new sport.*
>*Practice a random act of kindness.*
>*Plan a vacation.*
>*Plan a "date" with your spouse.*
>*Volunteer to work a few hours for a local charity.*
>*Buy tickets to attend a play.*
>*Send a "thinking of you" card to someone.*
>*Plan an activity for a group you work with.*
>   *Smile, smile, smile.*

J U N

15
June
16

GET OUT of a RUT in June

𝔊𝔬𝔩𝔡𝔢𝔫 ℜ𝔲𝔩𝔢 Habit

TODAY...   *I discover my habit to*
          GET OUT OF A RUT!

What do you think the view would be like from the bottom of a rut? When we're stuck in a rut, the view remains the same. What kind of fears and worries are keeping you down in the rut or behind the hurdle? What can you do to continue the joy and the journey of life?

>*Stop worrying about the potholes in the road*
>*and celebrate the journey!*
>FITZHUGH MULLAN, M.D. AND BARBARA HOFFMAN, CHARTING THE JOURNEY

A man's reach should exceed his grasp, or else what is heaven for?
ROBERT BROWNING, BRITISH POET

>*The only thing worse than failing is being afraid to try.*
>FRANK MINGO

Next time you're driving, go ahead – hit a pothole.
(Just a very little one. I don't want to be responsible for damaging your car.)

TODAY . . . **I discover my habit to**
 GET OUT OF A RUT!

Focusing on self-improvement wouldn't be complete without the topic of education. How many people are stuck in a rut without education? What education have you been putting off? Would you like to learn to sky dive, or to play a musical instrument? This month, June, it's time to spread your wings and fly!!!

Education's purpose is to replace an empty mind with an open one.
MALCOLM S. FORBES, AMERICAN BUSINESSMAN

Where there is an open mind, there will always be a frontier.
CHARLES F. KETTERING

Find at least one educational brochure and sign up to take a course.

Golden Rule Habit

GET OUT
of a
R**U**T
in June

17
June
18

J
U
N

TODAY . . . **I discover my habit to**
 GET OUT OF A RUT!

One of the best ways to stay in a rut is to procrastinate.
Close your eyes for a minute and think about the issues
in your own life. Where do you feel stress?
Is the stress coming from something you should be doing and don't?
Here's a quote with a little humor to speed your actions along.

When you wait,
all that happens is that you get older.
LARRY MCMURTRY, SOME CAN WHISTLE

If opportunity doesn't knock – build a door.
MILTON BERLE, AMERICAN COMEDIAN

Use five free minutes to start building the door to a new project.

TODAY ... **I discover my habit to**
GET OUT OF A RUT!

This month we celebrate Father's Day. I read the quote below about growing up and laughed because it describes parenting as well as childhood. So few of us have ever taken parenting courses. We parent with "How?" instead of "Know-How." We lead with our hearts and hope our "series of advances" produce healthy, well-adjusted children. Of all life's roles, parenting is one that is hard to do from down in a rut. We honor and appreciate you – DAD; it's a difficult job.

> *Growing up doesn't have to be so much a straight line*
> *as a series of advances.*
> KEVIN ARNOLD, "THE WONDER YEARS"

> *Life is at it's best when it's shaken and stirred.*
> F. PAUL FACULTE

Send cards or greetings to
your favorite father(s)!!

JUN

19
June
20

GET OUT of a RUT in June

Golden Rule Habit

TODAY ... **I discover my habit to**
GET OUT OF A RUT!

I found the following two quotes and discovered that they go together. If we just turn the stumbling block into stepping stones and then lay them across the river that looks a hundred miles wide...we will reach our dreams on the other side – OF COURSE. It will be easy.

> *...That river looks a hundred miles wide*
> *When all your dreams are on the other side.*
> BARRY MANILOW, SINGER, "BROOKLYN BLUES"

> *One of the secrets of life is to make stepping stones*
> *out of stumbling blocks.*
> JACK PENN

When it rains, watch the individual raindrops fall – think of oceans.

TODAY... *I discover my habit to*
GET OUT OF A RUT!

Look ahead to the joyous journey of a new day. Today, you have 1,440 minutes to shine and to make a difference. If you want to look back now and then, look back to the month of May. Remember to be appreciative, and thankful for each tiny moment we have, every day.

> *Don't look back.*
> *Something may be gaining on you.*
> SATCHEL (LEROY) PAIGE, FORMER BASEBALL PLAYER, HOW TO KEEP YOUNG

Take an extra moment of preparation to look your best
in honor of the new day.

Golden Rule Habit

GET OUT of a RUT in June

21 June **22**

J U N

TODAY... *I discover my habit to*
GET OUT OF A RUT!

Everything man-made is created out of the thoughts and dreams of someone. Every building; every light bulb; every popsicle stick; every box of chocolate cake mix; every paper clip; every clock; every jelly bean; and every hula hoop; began as a dream of possibility in the mind of one person.

It is said that a man's life can be measured by the dreams he fulfills.
MR. ROARKE, "FANTASY ISLAND"

Don't wait for your ship to come in. Swim out to it.
AUTHOR UNKNOWN

I like the dreams of the future better than the history of the past.
THOMAS JEFFERSON, THIRD PRESIDENT OF THE UNITED STATES

Make room in your life to begin your dream(s).

134

TODAY ...   *I discover my habit to*
GET OUT OF A RUT!

Take today off.

"Forget" to pick-up your e:mail and messages.
  Enjoy one of your "ruts" for the last time.

TODAY ...   *I discover my habit to*
GET OUT OF A RUT!

There have always been great explorers among us. Perhaps it's
because there's a fascination in the act of thrusting forward and
traveling to new places or making new discoveries. Sometimes
the challenge is like going through a door, simply because you find
the door in front of you. You have no idea what is on the other side,
but you take the risk to find out.

> *I think that man loses something, if he has the option*
> *to go to the moon and does not take it.*
>
> NEIL ARMSTRONG, MICHAEL COLLINS AND EDWIN ALDRIN,
> AMERICAN ASTRONAUTS, FIRST ON THE MOON

If you haven't already, learn to get on the internet
– or learn something new about the internet.

TODAY . . . *I discover my habit to*
GET OUT OF A RUT!

This quote is beautiful and completes our inspiration for the day.
If it's too late for the sunrise, then watch the sunset
– all the way down until you can't see it anymore. Just do it.

> *Climb up on a hill at sunrise.*
> *Everybody needs perspective once in a while,*
> *and you'll find it there.*
> ROBB SAGENDORPH

> *Only you have the power to change IMPOSSIBLE*
> *to mean... I'M POSSIBLE!*
> DARLENE PATRICK

Watch a sunrise or a sunset today.

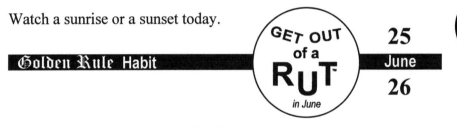

Golden Rule Habit

GET OUT of a RUT in June

25 June 26

J
U
N.

TODAY . . . *I discover my habit to*
GET OUT OF A RUT!

We've been working on building our own courage to follow dreams
this month. Today the question is, *"Are there other people in your life
with dreams?"* The next question is, *"Can you help them achieve their
dreams?"* Each day we are a part of the dream-building process for
our own children. Through us, they learn to look up, or to look down.

> *As we make it,*
> *we've got to reach back*
> *and pull up those left behind.*
> JOSHUA L. SMITH

Help a child with a problem or
help someone solve a dilemma they are facing.

TODAY . . .   ***I discover my habit to***
                 GET OUT OF A RUT!

Dreams are the stuff that life is made of. Read again, the Langston Hughes poem at the beginning of the chapter.

> *Everything starts as somebody's daydream.*
> LARRY NIVEN, NIVEN'S LAWS

Dreams are necessary to life.
ANAIS NIN

> *A world without dreams and hopes is no world at all.*
> ARETHA FRANKLIN, AMERICAN SINGER

> *The wild dreams of today are the practical realities of tomorrow.*
> CAPTAIN CRANE, "VOYAGE TO THE BOTTOM OF THE SEA"

Dream of being different...serve a backwards meal – starting with dessert.

27
June
28

J
U
N

𝕲𝖔𝖑𝖉𝖊𝖓 𝕽𝖚𝖑𝖊 Habit

TODAY . . .   ***I discover my habit to***
                 GET OUT OF A RUT!

Make total health a "Get Out of a Rut" goal for yourself and your family.

> *The key to exercising a family*
> *isn't to get the kids to work out like adults,*
> *it's to get the parents to play like the kids.*
> AUTHOR UNKNOWN

If you fatten up every one around you, you will look thinner yourself.
AUTHOR UNKNOWN

> *Parsley is a decoration that diverts your attention*
> *from the small size of the entree.*
> AUTHOR UNKNOWN

Serve dinner on a saucer. Eat VERY slowly. Enjoy each bite.

TODAY...   *I discover my habit to*
GET OUT OF A RUT!

This month you've opened your eyes to some new possibilities in your own life. I hope you've discovered the joy of breaking new ground and of getting un-stuck from attitudes or actions that haven't brought you the happiness you deserve.

> *If a window of opportunity appears,*
> *don't pull down the shade.*
> TOM PETERS, THE PURSUIT OF WOW!

We are born with our eyes closed and our mouths open,
and we spend our whole lives
trying to reverse that mistake of nature.
DALE E. TURNER

When driving home today, deliberately take a wrong turn and see what's down that road.

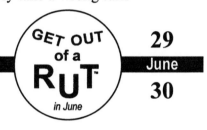

𝕲𝖔𝖑𝖉𝖊𝖓 𝕽𝖚𝖑𝖊 Habit

GET OUT of a **R**U**T** in June

29
June
30

JUN

TODAY...   *I discover my habit to*
GET OUT OF A RUT!

Today is the last day of June – it's a great day to bring up the ghastly idea of defeat and quitting. Today is NOT the day to quit getting out of your rut. Today is the day to re-commit yourself, to all the great projects or promises you made to yourself, to achieve your dreams. You might even promise yourself to get started on a few more.

> *Being defeated is often a temporary condition.*
> *Giving up is what makes it permanent.*
> MARILYN VOS SAVANT

> *You're never a loser until you quit trying.*
> MIKE DITKA, HEAD COACH, NEW ORLEANS SAINTS

If at first you don't succeed try again and again,
but above all, never quit.

CHAPTER 7

Color "Cue" - Patriot Red

"Together We Can Brighten the World We All Share."

IN JULY, I WILL REMEMBER TO...
BECOME INVOLVED

July is flavored with love of country. It is a month of family and neighborhood gatherings. "Patriot Red" is the color of the American Spirit and of nationalism. It's a good time to think about your community and to consider your own role in it.

If you aren't vacationing this month, then you might have a little extra time to find an organization nearby to become involved with as a volunteer. Perhaps you can help with something going on in the neighborhood; a garage sale or a food kitchen sponsored by a local charity.

Getting involved as a volunteer helps others, but it also helps you. This is why working as a volunteer for Habitat for Humanity has become so popular. Families get new houses built by volunteers – but the volunteers get the shared joy of working together side-by-side, on a common task that has purpose and meaning.

This age of television takes time from our lives that we used to spend just being together with others and working on common tasks that help our communities. Think about taking some time from your busy life to give away.

Many parents are involved together with summer youth sports like little league. Look in the community section of the newspaper. Maybe the Boy Scouts are planning an event, or better still an old-fashioned camp out. Organizations and ideas for volunteering will be shared with you each day this month. People who become involved make a caring difference. Become involved.

Goal for the Month:

>Have a great summer by volunteering some of your time
>to your community.

"Together We Can Brighten the World We All Share."

The Ripple Effect

AUTHOR UNKNOWN

Drop a stone into the water
In a moment it is gone,
Yet there are a hundred ripples
Circling on and on.

Say an unkind word this moment,
In a moment it is gone,
Yet there are a hundred ripples
Circling on and on.

Say a word of cheer and splendor
In a moment it is gone,
Yet there are a hundred ripples
Circling on and on.

TODAY . . .   *I honor my habit to*
BECOME INVOLVED

> *God created us so that we should form the human family,*
> *existing together because we were made for one another.*
> *We are not made for an exclusive self-sufficiency, but for*
> *interdependence, and we break this law of being at our peril.*
>
> DESMOND TUTU, SOUTH AFRICAN EPISCOPAL BISHOP

> *If we do not lay out ourselves in the service of mankind*
> *whom should we serve?*
>
> ABIGAIL ADAMS, FORMER FIRST LADY

> *In a world where there is so much to be done,*
> *I feel strongly impressed*
> *that there must be something for me to do.*
>
> DOROTHEA DIX

Volunteer in a summer school or classroom.

𝕲𝖔𝖑𝖉𝖊𝖓 𝕽𝖚𝖑𝖊 Habit   **become involved** *in July*   **1** July **2**

J U L

TODAY . . .   *I honor my habit to*
BECOME INVOLVED

What are some excuses for not getting involved? Maybe it's because it rains, or it's too hot, or it's too cold, or you don't have enough time right now, or you are poor, or no one invited you, or you'll miss your favorite TV program, or your clothes are not expensive, or because you really WILL do it LATER.

> *Turn off the TV, turn off the CD player,*
> *and do something for your family,*
> *for your community,*
> *for yourself.*
>
> MICKY DOLENZ, AMERICAN SINGER-ACTOR, THE MONKEES, I'M A BELIEVER

Volunteer or just visit a nursing home.

144

TODAY . . . ***I honor my habit to***
BECOME INVOLVED

Don't quote me on this – but I read somewhere that less than 20% of the people in America are involved as volunteers. Yet, there is so much suffering – it's easy to see that all of us are needed to help out in some way. What would happen if the other 80% gave time to help others? Which percent are you?

> *One of America's biggest problems is not simply bad people who do wrong, but good people who do nothing.*
> TED LINDMAN

> *If you're not part of the solution, you're part of the problem.*
> ELDRIDGE CLEAVER

Babysit for a neighborhood mother who needs a few hours to herself.

3
July

become
in**volved**
in July

𝔊𝔬𝔩𝔡𝔢𝔫 𝔕𝔲𝔩𝔢 Habit

4

TODAY . . . ***I honor my habit to***
BECOME INVOLVED

Today is the Fourth of July. On this day we all remember to stay home from work and to find the nearest fireworks display. Let's remember too – that our Declaration of Independence was signed on July 4, 1776. What if our forefathers had not become involved in the pursuit of freedom and liberty? They risked their lives to sign a document that founded the United States of America.

> *And so, my fellow Americans, ask not what your country can do for you – ask what you can do for your country.*
> *My fellow citizens of the world, ask not what America will do for you, but what we together will do for the freedom of man.*
> JOHN F. KENNEDY, 35TH PRESIDENT OF THE UNITED STATES

Is there a community event or a festival that could use your help?

TODAY . . . *I honor my habit to*
BECOME INVOLVED

Sometimes "becoming involved" takes courage. How many crimes are prevented by people who have the courage to step in and help? How many crimes succeed because people don't do anything? It took courage to lead our nation to freedom from British tyranny in 1776. Sometimes it takes courage to help a friend by telling them your honest opinion of their actions or deeds.

With a firm reliance on the protection of Divine Providence,
we mutually pledge to each other our lives,
our fortunes, and our sacred honor.
THOMAS JEFFERSON, THIRD PRESIDENT OF THE UNITED STATES
THE DECLARATION OF INDEPENDENCE

Participate in Block Watch or a neighborhood safety program.

TODAY . . . *I honor my habit to*
BECOME INVOLVED

Just "speaking" up is sometimes all it takes to become involved and to make a difference. Is there something going on in your life that needs you to speak up?

In Germany, the Nazis came for the Communists, and I didn't speak up because I was not a Communist. Then they came for the Jews, and I didn't speak up because I was not a Jew. Then they came for the trade unionists and I did not speak up because I was not a trade unionist. Then they came for the Catholics and I was a Protestant so I did not speak up. Then they came for me. By that time, there was no one left to speak up for anyone.
MARTIN NIEMOLLER

Get involved with a community service organization
like the Kiwanis or Rotary.

TODAY . . .   *I honor my habit to*
BECOME INVOLVED

Why wait for tragedies to happen before we get involved? Why let "getting involved" slip away after the urgency of a disaster has dissipated? If you have become involved because of an immediate tragedy or disaster – turn the motivation into a long-term habit to – STAY involved. Your community needs you at all times.

> *Motivation is what gets you started.*
> *Habit is what keeps you going.*
> JIM RYUN, AMERICAN DISTANCE RUNNER

> *To say, yes, you have to sweat and roll up your sleeves*
> *and plunge both hands into life up to the elbows.*
> *It is easier to say no.*
> JEAN ANOUILH

Volunteer with the Red Cross.

7 July

8

JUL

become **involved** *in July*

𝕮𝖔𝖑𝖉𝖊𝖓 𝕽𝖚𝖑𝖊 Habit

TODAY . . .   *I honor my habit to*
BECOME INVOLVED

The gift of our environment is a treasure we too often take for granted. Our founding fathers wrote a "Bill of Rights" but not a "Bill of Responsibilities." Our rights include responsibilities that can't be ignored, if our communities are to thrive. Consider the hungry birds in winter or an endangered animal species. They need human support to remain among us so that our children may know and enjoy them someday.

> *Say 'Yes' to the seedlings and a giant forest cleaves the sky.*
> *Say 'Yes' to the universe and the planets become your neighbors.*
> *Say 'Yes' to dreams of love and freedom.*
> *It is the password to utopia.*
> BROOKS ATKINSON

Find an environmental cause and take action – or simply plant a tree. Take your family to the zoo.

TODAY . . .   *I honor my habit to*
BECOME INVOLVED

One of the neatest truths is that "volunteering" is both noble and self-ish. In recent years, Habitat for Humanity has become one of the most popular volunteer organizations in America. They know that there is joy in working together with others. Rubbing the shoulder of a fellow volunteer as you work side by side, can be one of the sweetest moments of the day. Be selfish. Become a volunteer.

> *The great difference between voyages rests not*
> *with the ships, but with the people you meet on them.*
> AMELIA BARR, ALL THE DAYS OF MY LIFE

Volunteer with Habitat for Humanity.
Experience the joy of working together for good.

Golden Rule Habit   become in**volved** in July   9 July 10

TODAY . . .   *I honor my habit to*
BECOME INVOLVED

Imagine what it would be like if you couldn't enjoy the rich adventure of reading. In your own community, there are people who cannot read. If reading is a special enjoyment of yours – then perhaps helping an adult or a child with reading skills would bring you pleasure too. Share your love of reading. Become involved.

> *Through books...ideas find their way to the human brains,*
> *and ideals to human hearts and souls.*
> DOROTHY CANFIELD FISHER

> *Five years from now, you will be pretty much the same*
> *as you are today except for two things:*
> *the books you read and the people you get close to.*
> CHARLES JONES

Volunteer in an adult literacy program or read to a child.

148

TODAY ...   ***I honor my habit to***
                 BECOME INVOLVED

Ask a teacher how you can make a difference while lying on your own bed. Teachers will tell you that many papers are graded, many a lesson plans written and many tests are scored during those "ought to be my own time" moments, even in bed. What time "ought to be your own"? When is it better to give time away?

> *I think even lying on my bed I can still do something.*
> DOROTHEA DIX

While lying in bed...
think about how you would like to make a caring difference.

become involved *in July*

𝔊𝔬𝔩𝔡𝔢𝔫 𝔎𝔲𝔩𝔢 Habit

TODAY ...   ***I honor my habit to***
                 BECOME INVOLVED

The arts help touch the heart and interpret those deep shared "knowings" that bring us together in spirit and love. Music and art can change our perspective and blend our points of view into one perspective of beauty.

> *The artistic innovator is perhaps our society's most valuable citizen. He or she does not so much change the world, as change how we view it. They are ambassadors of peace and advocates of understanding. They melt our differences into the common ground of the dance floor, the theater, the concert hall, and a million living rooms across the nation. That is why it is important that we so diligently search for them.*
> OSSIE DAVIS, AMERICAN ACTOR

Volunteer to help the arts – support a theater, orchestra or art museum.

TODAY...   *I honor my habit to*
BECOME INVOLVED

We are a country of enthusiastic sports spectators – which is great. We aren't all qualified to play, and yet we can all enjoy the thrill of winning. When it comes to making a difference and getting involved, however, there is a place or two – down on the field – that each of us needs to fill. When we don't take our position, someone or something somewhere, loses.

> *You must get involved to make an impact.*
> *No one is impressed with the won-lost record*
> *of the referee.*
> JOHN H. HOLCOMB, THE MILITANT MODERATE

Volunteer to coach or help out a children's sports team.

ᛟᚱᛚᛞᛖᚾ Rule Habit   **become involved** *in July*   **13** July **14**

TODAY...   *I honor my habit to*
BECOME INVOLVED

It seems like our American motto has become "more is better." When was the last time you bought an item of clothing that you actually needed? I know I will never really need a new dress. What would happen to hunger and poverty if we all focused on making a difference more than on making more money? They are not mutually exclusive and they can both be done and done well. There is a book by L. Lawrence Embley available at the library entitled, *Doing Well While Doing Good.* If you have some time, check it out.

> *Our greatness is built upon our freedom.*
> *It is moral, not material. We have a great ardor for gain:*
> *but we have a deep passion for the rights of man.(woman)*
> WOODROW WILSON, 28TH PRESIDENT OF THE UNITED STATES

Volunteer at a shelter or a soup kitchen. Notice that "less isn't so great."

150

TODAY... **I honor my habit to**
BECOME INVOLVED

One of the problems with a democracy is that someone always gets elected even if they don't represent most of the people. This happens when eligible voters don't vote. Then they are not represented. Become involved in making sure you know who is running for political offices and then get out and vote.

He serves his party best who serves his country best.
RUTHERFORD B. HAYES, 19TH PRESIDENT OF THE UNITED STATES

A politician thinks of the next election;
a statesman thinks of the next generation.
JAMES FREEMAN CLARKE

Plan to volunteer at a voting booth in your ward or precinct – and of course – VOTE.

15
July

become **involved**
in July

Golden Rule Habit

16

JUL

TODAY... **I honor my habit to**
BECOME INVOLVED

Mental reminders and practice won't replace involvement that is motivated from within your heart and spirit. This is what "being connected" is all about. Think about your relationships with your family and friends or with your worship community. Today, think deeply, from your heart and spirit. Look at others from your heart. What do you see?

Trust in God and do something.
MARY LYON

The gift you have received,
give as a gift.

MATTHEW 10:8, NEW AMERICAN BIBLE

Become involved with your church or place of worship or of service.

TODAY . . . *I honor my habit to*
BECOME INVOLVED

I saw a "GOLDEN RULE" billboard the other day – I wish I knew who put it there. It held the following message displayed as though it were signed by God. It read,
> *"That love thy neighbor thing... I meant that." —GOD*

> *The condition upon which God hath given*
> *liberty to man is eternal vigilance.*
> JOHN PHILPOT CURRAN

Walk down the street today with love in your heart
for your neighbor.

TODAY . . . *I honor my habit to*
BECOME INVOLVED

If there were no drops there would be no ocean. As one person, it is easy not to get involved because you think you can't make a difference. Think about this. How many people did you interact with in some way today? If you left your home at all – your answer is probably between ten and twenty or more. In a week this number reaches to more than 100 and in a month...well, you get the point. Were all of your interactions caring and pleasant? Could you have made more of a positive difference than you did?

We ourselves feel that what we are doing is just a drop in the ocean.
But the ocean would be less because of that missing drop.
> MOTHER TERESA, FOUNDER, MISSIONARIES OF CHARITY

Add "something better" to each of your interactions today,
even if just a smile.

152

TODAY... **I honor my habit to**
            BECOME INVOLVED

Sometimes there's a fine line between the activist who gets involved by speaking up for change – and the "all talk" naysayer who never makes things better – only worse – with the noise of his voice. Be an "activist" for what you believe in – support a positive plan for improvement.

> *The human race is divided into two classes*
> *– those who go ahead and do something and those who sit*
> *still and inquire, 'Why wasn't it done the other way?'*
> OLIVER WENDELL HOLMES, AMERICAN AUTHOR

Attend a community meeting where an important issue is in discussion. Add your constructive opinion, volunteer for a research committee, or do research on your own.

19 July **20** become in**volved**™ in July   𝕲𝖔𝖑𝖉𝖊𝖓 𝕽𝖚𝖑𝖊 Habit

JUL

TODAY... **I honor my habit to**
            BECOME INVOLVED

Activism, is often not popular. It threatens people's comfort zones. When great changes have been needed in our democratic society – the courageous people suffer greatly. Rosa Parks sat down at the front of a bus for what was right – equality.

> *I want every American free to stand up for his rights,*
> *even if sometimes he has to sit down for them.*
> JOHN F. KENNEDY, 35TH PRESIDENT OF THE UNITED STATES

> *To sin by silence when they should protest*
> *makes cowards out of men.*
> ABRAHAM LINCOLN, 16TH PRESIDENT OF THE UNITED STATES

If you believe in an issue, take a stand for it – even if it's unpopular.

TODAY... *I honor my habit to*
BECOME INVOLVED

In this patriotic month of July, with 20 days of "become involved" behind us – it's time to increase the pressure a little. Add the thought that becoming involved is more than something nice to do. It is a responsibility. Every person must become involved as a voter and as a steward of freedom so that democracy works for everyone – not just for the people with power.

> *What you ought to do, you should do;*
> *and what you should do, you ought to do!*
> OPRAH WINFREY, AMERICAN TALK-SHOW HOSTESS AND ACTRESS

> *Honey, it's so easy to talk a good game.*
> *What we need are folks who will do something.*
> MAXINE WATERS, AMERICAN GOSPEL SINGER

Spend one hour today, (60 minutes) making a difference. You're free. You decide how.

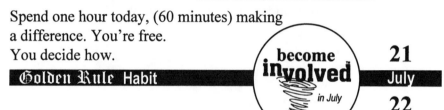

𝔊𝔬𝔩𝔡𝔢𝔫 𝔎𝔲𝔩𝔢 Habit

become inVolved *in July*

21
July
22

J
U
L

TODAY... *I honor my habit to*
BECOME INVOLVED

One of the best things about becoming involved – is that the influence of your effort is multiplied. Remember the poem at the beginning of this month. Have you ever dropped a stone into a pond and watched the ripples?

> *All work is as seed sown;*
> *it grows and spreads, and sows itself anew.*
> THOMAS CARLYLE

> *That's what being young is all about. You have the courage*
> *and the daring to think that you can make a difference.*
> RUBY DEE, AMERICAN ACTRESS

Volunteer to do fundraising for the United Way.

154

TODAY . . . **_I honor my habit to_**
           BECOME INVOLVED

My father taught me everything I ever needed to know about service. At age 91, he just received the Humanitarian of the Year Award in his community. He had already won this award in the hearts of his family years ago. Thank You to my Dad...Earl Stevens.

> *Service is where love is.*
> *Our work brings people face to face with love.*
> MOTHER TERESA, FOUNDER, MISSIONARIES OF CHARITY

> *It is by believing, hoping, loving, and doing*
> *that man finds joy and peace.*
> JOHN LANCASTER SPALDING

Call the Salvation Army and sign up to volunteer now.

23 July **24**

become **involved** *in July*

𝕲𝖔𝖑𝖉𝖊𝖓 𝕽𝖚𝖑𝖊 Habit

J U L

TODAY . . . **_I honor my habit to_**
           BECOME INVOLVED

A few days ago, I suggested you spend one hour making a difference. Civic commitment is even better when it's long term. (Ret.) General Colin Powell heads America's Promise – Alliance for Youth. There are many opportunities to volunteer with them, from becoming a mentor, to starting an after school program for teens.

> *Those who expect to reap the blessings of freedom*
> *must undergo the fatigue of supporting it.*
> THOMAS PAINE

> *A community is like a ship;*
> *everyone ought to be prepared to take the helm.*
> HENRIK IBSEN, NORWEGIAN PLAYWRIGHT, AN ENEMY OF THE PEOPLE

Contact America's Promise at (703) 684-4500
or website: www.americaspromise.org

TODAY... **I honor my habit to**
BECOME INVOLVED

Serve quietly.

> *The world is divided into people who do things*
> *and people who get the credit.*
> *Try, if you can, to belong to the first class.*
> *There's far less competition.*
>> DWIGHT MORROW

> *Be a fountain, not a drain.*
>> REX HUDLER

Make an anonymous contribution to your favorite charity.

𝕲𝖔𝖑𝖉𝖊𝖓 𝕽𝖚𝖑𝖊 Habit become in**volved** in July **25** July **26**

J U L

TODAY... **I honor my habit to**
BECOME INVOLVED

Our youth are 20% of the present and 100% of our future. You are 100% of your own future. Your future, and mine, and our children's – starts in the next second.

> *Our sons and daughters must be trained in national service,*
> *taught to give as well as to receive.*
>> EMMELINE PANKHURST

> *We should all be concerned about the future because*
> *we will have to spend the rest of our lives there.*
>> CHARLES F. KETTERING, SEED FOR THOUGHT

Call the Volunteer Centers Hotline for
"Point a kid in the right direction" – 1-888-559-6884

156

TODAY...　　**I honor my habit to**
　　　　　　　　BECOME INVOLVED

There are many young people today who have never heard of Helen Keller. (1880-1968). Blind and deaf from birth, she learned to speak, read and write. She traveled and lectured to millions of people around the world. She became an inspiration for what one person, who is courageous and determined – can do.

> *Do not let what you cannot do*
> *interfere with what you can do.*
> JOHN WOODEN, FORMER BASKETBALL COACH, U.C.L.A., THEY CALL ME COACH

You give but little when you give one of your possessions.
It is when you give of yourself that you truly give.
　　　　　　KAHLIL GIBRAN, THE PROPHET

Consider volunteering at a school for the handicapped or at a blind center.

27 July **28**

become **involved** *in July*

𝔊𝔬𝔩𝔡𝔢𝔫 𝔕𝔲𝔩𝔢 Habit

JUL

TODAY...　　**I honor my habit to**
　　　　　　　　BECOME INVOLVED

I recently heard a lecture by Wayne Dyer, a nationally known lecturer and author. He shared a secret with us. He has a suit in his closet with the pockets cut off. He keeps this suit there to remind him that when he "goes" – he won't take it with him. Not one of us owns anything – except our own heart and soul.

> *We are here to add what we can to,*
> *not to get what we can from, life.*
> SIR WILLIAM OSLER

As for me, prizes mean nothing. My prize is my work.
　　　　KATHARINE HEPBURN, AMERICAN ACTRESS, KATE

We work to become, not to acquire.
ELBERT HUBBARD

Take the next check that comes in the mail and give it away.

TODAY... ***I honor my habit to***
BECOME INVOLVED

I heard a remarkable story about the funeral of a man from Columbia, SC. Apparently he had written a book *The Secret of a Happy Life,* but had not sold any copies. His wish was to have the book distributed at his funeral. He was a happy man who was loved by many throughout his life. The funeral was attended by hundreds of grateful mourners and the greatly anticipated book was passed out at the end of the ceremony. Most likely it became the first book in history to ever be read in its entirety by every recipient. Written inside the book was one word. "SERVICE."

> *The roots of happiness grow best in the soil of service.*
> RUTH B. LOVE

While you are volunteering, look into the faces around you and know you are appreciated.

Golden Rule Habit — **become involved** *in July* — **29** July **30**

TODAY... ***I honor my habit to***
BECOME INVOLVED

How will you measure success in your life? Take time to step back from the crowd – the crowd that values making a killing on the stock market, or beating out a partner in a deal. There IS great value in capitalism, democracy and in the America Dream – as long as it is not a disguise for America Greed. Accumulate the riches of service, love, family and friends.

> *I must admit that I personally measure success*
> *in terms of the contributions an individual makes*
> *to his or her fellow human beings.*
> MARGARET MEAD, AMERICAN ANTHROPOLOGIST

Does a family member or friend need some help?
Can you find time to get involved?

TODAY . . .   ***I honor my habit to***
                                   BECOME INVOLVED

It's the last day of July, our monthly habit-building assessment day. If you are already a volunteer or a regular charity supporter or work on a cause that is important to you, then praise be to you. Thank goodness for you – you are playing your part in the larger picture of community. If you have not made such a commitment – please evaluate the idea of volunteering once again. Somehow, somewhere, you are needed and you can make a caring difference.

> *Happiness consists of activity*
> *– it is a running stream, not a stagnant pool.*
> JOHN MASON GOOD

> *It's easy to make a buck.*
> *It's a lot tougher*
> *to make a difference.*
> TOM BROKAW, AMERICAN JOURNALIST

> *If anyone thinks he has no responsibilities,*
> *it is because he has not sought them out.*
> MARY LYON

> *We cannot do everything at once,*
> *but we can do something at once.*
> CALVIN COOLIDGE, 30TH PRESIDENT OF THE UNITED STATES

> *Teach this triple truth to all:*
>   *a generous heart, kind speech, and a life of service*
>   *and compassion are the things which renew humanity.*
> BUDDHA

Either thank yourself for the service you do – or think again about seeking out your own special way to become involved.

CHAPTER 8

Color "Cue" - Thoughtful Blue

"Together We Can Brighten the World We All Share."

160

IN AUGUST, REMEMBER TO...
KNOW WHO I AM

This above all, to thine own self be true
And it must follow as the night the day
Thou canst not then be false to any man.

WILLIAM SHAKESPEARE, BRITISH PLAYWRIGHT AND POET, HAMLET

August is the summation of the GOLDEN RULE REVOLUTION –
the month to evaluate who you are and how well you "walk your own
talk." August is a month of vacations – a time to relax and also to
reflect. Your habit-building color for this month is "Thoughtful Blue."
Encourage yourself, in August, to reflect on who you are, and where
"you" are taking your own future. What kind of memories are you
making out of your own moments?

Who are you, how are you different from a year ago – and how do you
want to be different a year from now? Reflect on your priorities, your
direction and your values. Do you allocate your time to support what is
important to you?

With appreciation to the Ty Ling Fortune Cookie Company, I have
ended each August day's inspiration with a fortune cookie philosophy
message. They are very thought provoking and can inspire a fleeting
moment of introspection. You may reflect on the messages I have chosen, or you might want to buy your own box of Fortune Cookies, and
reflect on one message each day. You may also prefer to use Scripture
passages or another source of meditation.

<u>Goal for the Month</u>:

> Be able to write down your own values about family, children
> personal behavior, work performance and your role in your
> community.

"Together We Can Brighten the World We All Share"

Truths for Living

WILLIAM ARTHUR WARD

The more generous we are,
the more joyous we become.

The more cooperative we are,
the more valuable we become.

The more enthusiastic we are,
the more productive we become.

The more serving we are,
the more prosperous we become.

The more outgoing we are,
the more helpful we become.

The more curious we are,
the more creative we become.

The more patient we are,
the more understanding we become.

The more persistent we are,
the more successful we become.

TODAY . . .   *I reflect on my habit to*
KNOW WHO I AM

"Treat others as you want others to treat you." This is the Golden Rule of mutual respect. This great principle for happiness is found in every great book of every great world religion. In a month dedicated to building the habit of self-reflection, this is a time to reflect on The Golden Rule and how each moment of your life supports the Rule.

> *Practicing the Golden Rule is not a sacrifice,*
> *it's an investment.*
> BYLLE AVERY

> *The rule of proportion.*
> ROBERT RECORDE

Fortune Cookie:
You are in for an enlightening experience.

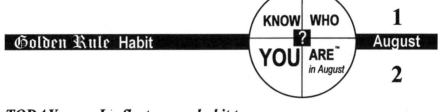

𝕲𝖔𝖑𝖉𝖊𝖓 𝕽𝖚𝖑𝖊 Habit

KNOW WHO **?** YOU ARE™ *in August*

1 August **2**

TODAY . . .   *I reflect on my habit to*
KNOW WHO I AM

A U G

Consider the idea that "prayer" is talking to God and "meditation" is listening. Inside each of us, is a conscience, known to many as God. When we listen to it, this inner voice guides us toward happiness. Practice both prayer and meditation this month. Read a meditation book, or simply quiet your own thoughts so that your inner-voice can be heard.

> *Two things hold me in awe: the starry heaven above me;*
> *and the moral law within me.*
> IMMANUEL KANT, PHILOSOPHER

> *Look well into thyself: there is a source of strength that will*
> *always spring up if thou wilt always look there.*
> MARCUS AURELIUS

Fortune Cookie: The courage to be great lies deep within each of us.

TODAY . . . **I reflect on my habit to**
KNOW WHO I AM

With more than 1,100 self-help books in current print, it is obvious that the search for happiness is a flourishing business. Why do we search for answers from someone else or in a book? Reflect on the answers to happiness that are inside of you now. How can you bring them alive in your own life?

Life is rather like a can of sardines – we're all looking for the key.
ALAN BENNET

Most people will search high and wide for the key to success.
If they only knew the key to their dreams lies within.
GEORGE WASHINGTON CARVER, AMERICAN SCIENTIST

Fortune Cookie: Your eyes will be opened to a world full of love, beauty and adventure.

TODAY . . . **I reflect on my habit to**
KNOW WHO I AM

There is no purpose in life more valuable than parenting. Today, reflect on who you are in the eyes of your children (of any age). What are you teaching them?

The best thing you can give your children are good values,
good memories and good food.
Good character, like good food, is usually homemade.
AUTHOR UNKNOWN

I tell Michael, 'Let them know what your priorities are: God, family, doing right, respect.' These are the things that are important in life.
DELORIS JORDAN, MOTHER OF BASKETBALL PLAYER, MICHAEL JORDAN

Fortune Cookie: A small gift can bring joy to the whole family.

TODAY . . .   I reflect on my habit to
KNOW WHO I AM

The best index to a person's character is
(a.) How (s)he treats people who can't do him (her) any good, and
(b.) How (s)he treats people who can't fight back.
ABIGAIL VAN BUREN, ADVICE COLUMNIST

One isn't born one's self. One is born with a mass of expectations,
a mass of other people's ideas – and you have to work through it all.
V. S. NAIPAUL

You have to start knowing yourself so well that you begin to know
other people. A piece of us is in every person we can ever meet.
JOHN D. MACDONALD

Fortune Cookie: You are open and honest in your philosophy of love.

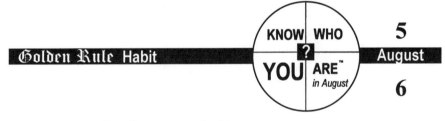

Golden Rule Habit | KNOW WHO YOU ARE™ in August | 5 August 6

TODAY . . .   I reflect on my habit to
KNOW WHO I AM

A
U
G

Did you know that less than 31% of the American public buys books
or has library cards? Have you outgrown your thirst for knowledge and
education as a source of personal fulfillment? What would you like to
learn more about? Why?

Education has for its object, the formation of character.
HERBERT SPENCER

It's not about who reaches the summit the fastest;
it's who learns the most about herself (himself) along the way.
BRANDI SHERWOOD, MISS U.S.A. 1997

There are...two educations. One should teach us how to
make a living and the other how to live.
JAMES TRUSLOW ADAMS

Fortune Cookie: Advancement will come with hard work.

TODAY ...   ***I reflect on my habit to***
KNOW WHO I AM

For many of us, reflecting on our mistakes is an obsession. People with low self-acceptance, often worry too much about what other people think of them. The question is, "Does your reflection make you feel bad or make you a better person in the future?"

> *When you make a mistake, admit it.*
> *If you don't, you only make matters worse.*
> <small>WARD CLEAVER, "LEAVE IT TO BEAVER"</small>

When you make a mistake, acknowledge it. Know that you cannot go back. Ask for pardon. Discover what you learned. Behave like you learned it. Go on, better than before.
<small>ELAINE PARKE</small>

Fortune Cookie: He who never makes mistakes never did anything that's worthy.

7

August

8

KNOW WHO **?** YOU ARE™ *in August*

Golden Rule Habit

A U G

TODAY ...   ***I reflect on my habit to***
KNOW WHO I AM

If I could back up the clock, I would re-program myself with the wisdom that, for better or for worse, our memories are the fabric of future thoughts. Memories haunt or hallow our minds – they depress or uplift our souls, they bring joy or sadness to our hearts.

> *Make the kind of memories that you can live with*
> *the rest of your life.*
> <small>AUTHOR UNKNOWN</small>

> *You never know when you're making a memory.*
> <small>EMPTY LEE JONES, AMERICAN SINGER, "YOUNG BLOOD"</small>

> *Remember wherever you go, there you are.*
> <small>PETER WELLER, "THE ADVENTURES OF BUCKAROO BONZI"</small>

Fortune Cookie: You must always have old memories and young hopes.

TODAY . . .   I reflect on my habit to
KNOW WHO I AM

What brand of car do you drive? What shoes do you wear?
What brand symbol is on your clothes? What is prestige?

> *If your idol is profit and pleasure, remember that man's*
> *value is not measured by what he has, but by what he is.*
> POPE JOHN PAUL II, ADDRESS TO INDIANS OF AMAZONIA, JUNE, 1980

No race can prosper till it learns that there is as much
dignity in tilling a field as in writing a poem.
BOOKER T. WASHINGTON, AUTHOR, UP FROM SLAVERY

> *I've always wanted to be somebody, but I see now*
> *I should have been more specific.*
> LILY TOMLIN, AMERICAN ACTRESS-COMEDIENNE,

Fortune Cookie:
How you look depends on where you go.

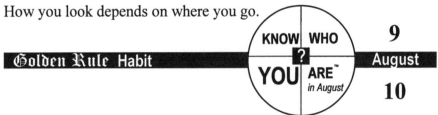

KNOW WHO **?** YOU ARE™ *in August* — **9** Golden Rule Habit August **10**

TODAY . . .   I reflect on my habit to
KNOW WHO I AM

What does success mean in your life?

> *Of all the qualities necessary for success,*
> *none comes before character.*
> ERNESTA PROCOPE

Success is always temporary. When all is said and done,
the only thing you'll have left is your character.
VINCE GILL, AMERICAN COUNTRY SINGER

> *You can have money and material things, but people*
> *– that's what really matters in life.*
> JOHN TRAVOLTA, AMERICAN ACTOR

Fortune Cookie: He who knows he has enough, is rich.

A
U
G

TODAY ...   ***I reflect on my habit to***
KNOW WHO I AM

Wouldn't it be neat to find an article in a woman's magazine about this kind of beauty?

*Character contributes to beauty. It fortifies a woman as her
 youth fades. A mode of conduct, a standard of courage,
 discipline, fortitude, and integrity can do a great deal
 to make a woman beautiful.*

JACQUELINE BISSETT, BRITISH ACTRESS

After a certain number of years, our faces become our biographies.

CYNTHIA OZICK, THE PARIS REVIEW

Good looks are no substitute for a sound character.

DOCTOR WHO, "DOCTOR WHO"

Fortune Cookie: Everything has beauty but not everyone sees it.

11
August

12

KNOW WHO
?
YOU ARE™
in August

𝕲𝖔𝖑𝖉𝖊𝖓 𝕽𝖚𝖑𝖊 Habit

TODAY ...   ***I reflect on my habit to***
KNOW WHO I AM

A
U
G

It doesn't take much self examination to know that we are not qualified to judge others. Then why do we spend so much time doing it? Take time this month to develop your ability to constructively criticize yourself.

*It is much more difficult to judge oneself
than to judge others.*

ANTOINE DE SAINT-EXUPERY, AUTHOR, THE LITTLE PRINCE

*Two things are bad for the heart
– running up stairs and running down people.*

BERNARD M. BARUCH, ISRALI STATESMAN

Fortune Cookie: The care and sensitivity you show towards others
will return to you.

TODAY ... **I reflect on my habit to**
KNOW WHO I AM

Psychologists and educators agree, that lack of self confidence and self-worth lies at the heart of many problems people have. Knowing yourself, increases your capacity for personal strength, and your chance for happiness.

> *A (wo)man cannot be comfortable*
> *without his/her own approval.*
> MARK TWAIN, AMERICAN AUTHOR AND ESSAYIST

> *Not all of us have to possess earth shaking talent.*
> *Just common sense and love will do.*
> MYRTLE AUVIL

Fortune Cookie: A friend is a present you give to yourself.

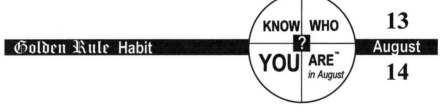

Golden Rule Habit | KNOW WHO YOU ARE™ *in August* | **13** August **14**

TODAY ... **I reflect on my habit to**
KNOW WHO I AM

A U G

Adversity strikes every life. The weak despair in the self-deception, that they alone, are dealt this hand of woe.

> *Only when a tree has fallen can you take the measure of it.*
> *It is the same with a man. (person.)*
> ANNE MORROW LINDBERGH, AMERICAN AUTHOR

> *One should look long and carefully*
> *at oneself before judging others.*
> MOLIERE, FRENCH PLAYWRIGHT

Fortune Cookie: Your doubts should disappear early this month.

TODAY . . . ***I reflect on my habit to***
KNOW WHO I AM

There is a "cumulative" quality to life, that's hard to conceptualize when you are young. Many regrets would probably be erased if we thought first, about the memories being made by our words and actions.

I am the master of my fate; I am the captain of my soul.
WILLIAM ERNEST HENLEY

Our deeds travel with us from afar.
And what we have been makes us what we are.
GEORGE ELIOT, BRITISH AUTHOR, MIDDLEMARCH

Every man is the son of his own words.
MIGUEL DE CERVANTES, SPANISH AUTHOR

Fortune Cookie: You are perceptive and considerate when dealing with others.

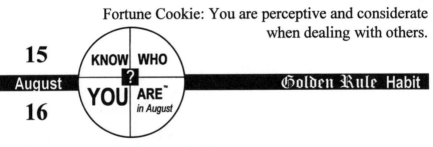

15 August 16

KNOW WHO YOU ARE™ in August

Golden Rule Habit

TODAY . . . ***I reflect on my habit to***
KNOW WHO I AM

Like our individual lives, the nature of society is also cumulative. Our social "norms" are created by the collective behaviors of the majority. Choosing to step out and volunteer your time, or to advocate for change is great – and needed. However, your contribution to a better world is also being made each day, with the words and actions of your own life.

One way to make the world better is by improving yourself.
WILLIE WILLIAMS, CHIEF OF POLICE, LOS ANGELES, CA

A human being's first responsibility is to shake hands with himself.
HENRY WINKLER, AMERICAN ACTOR

World economics without world ethics is very dangerous.
AUTHOR UNKNOWN

Fortune Cookie: The happiest circumstances are close to home.

TODAY... **I reflect on my habit to**
KNOW WHO I AM

We sometimes search for new answers to happiness while the answers sit, unpracticed, in our own minds and hearts.

Out of our beliefs are born deeds;
Out of our deeds we form habits;
Out of our habits grow our character;
And on our character we build our destiny.
HENRY HANCOCK

We can be thankful for what we have or complain about what we do not have. One or the other becomes a habit pattern of our own life.
ELISABETH ELLIOTT

Habits are first cobwebs, then cables.
SPANISH PROVERB

Fortune Cookie: The greater part of inspiration is perspiration.

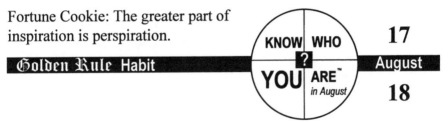

Golden Rule Habit

KNOW WHO
?
YOU ARE™
in August

17

August

18

A
U
G

TODAY... **I reflect on my habit to**
KNOW WHO I AM

Who's in charge of your life – a self-determined inspired you – or the random happenings of life.

We are free up to the point of choice.
Then the choice controls the chooser.
MARY CROWLEY

The vital, successful people I have met,
all had one common characteristic.
They had a plan.
MARILYN VAN DERBUR, MISS AMERICA 1958

Fortune Cookie: Don't wait for others to open the right door for you.

TODAY . . . **I reflect on my habit to**
KNOW WHO I AM

For centuries, the issue of temptation has been at the heart of good and evil choices. Temptation is powerful. The progress of inspired morality throughout society has therefore, been slow. Perhaps the search for new answers to happiness goes on because we don't exercise the self-discipline needed to practice time-honored answers, like the Golden Rule.

Temptation is sure to ring your doorbell,
but don't ask it to stay for dinner.
AUTHOR UNKNOWN

A talent is formed in stillness, a character in the world's torrent.
JOHANN WOLFGANG VON GOETHE, GERMAN AUTHOR

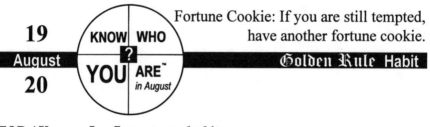

19
August
20

KNOW WHO
?
YOU ARE™
in August

Fortune Cookie: If you are still tempted, have another fortune cookie.

𝔊𝔬𝔩𝔡𝔢𝔫 𝔯𝔲𝔩𝔢 Habit

TODAY . . . **I reflect on my habit to**
KNOW WHO I AM

A
U
G

Instead of harping on a man's (person's) faults, tell him of his
virtues. Try to pull him out of his rut of bad habits. Hold him up
to his better self, his real self that can dare and do and win out!...
The influence of a beautiful, helpful, hopeful character
is contagious, and may revolutionize a whole town
...People radiate what is in their minds and in their hearts.
ELEANOR H. PORTER, AMERICAN AUTHOR, POLLYANNA

Some people change jobs, spouses, and friends
– but never think of changing themselves.
PAULA GIDDINGS

Fortune Cookie:
Your skills will accomplish what the force of many cannot.

TODAY...   *I reflect on my habit to*
KNOW WHO I AM

Look around you. Unless you are in the woods surrounded by pure nature, you are surrounded by items that were once ideas and beliefs that began in someone's mind and heart. Every great invention was at first a frail idea. What do you believe in?
What frail idea can you contribute?

We are what we believe we are.
BENJAMIN N. CARDOZO

In search of my mother's garden, I found my own.
ALICE WALKER, AMERICAN AUTHOR

Fortune Cookie: Being the first to try something new could make you great.

KNOW WHO **?** YOU ARE™ *in August*

Golden Rule Habit

21 August **22**

A U G

TODAY...   *I reflect on my habit to*
KNOW WHO I AM

Keep a balance in life between pride and humility. Knowing yourself helps keep that balance steady, despite what happens day to day.

Life is a long lesson in humility.
SIR JAMES M. BARRIE, BRITISH AUTHOR, THE LITTLE MINISTER

Success can make you go one of two ways. It can make you a prima donna, or it can smooth the edges, take away the insecurities, let the nice things come out.
BARBARA WALTERS, AMERICAN JOURNALIST

Fortune Cookie:
Do not let great ambitions overshadow small successes.

TODAY... **I reflect on my habit to**
KNOW WHO I AM

Reverence and awe are a great source of joy. A sense of blissful wonder about the greatness of God, is what spiritual commitment is about. Reverence is our best source of humility.
How can ego reign in the presence of God?

> *If a man loses reverence for any part of life,*
> *he will soon lose reverence for all life.*
> ALBERT SCHWEITZER, PHYSICIAN

> *Our life is a faint tracing on the surface of mystery.*
> ANNIE DILLARD

> *The things that we love tell us what we are.*
> ST. THOMAS AQUINAS

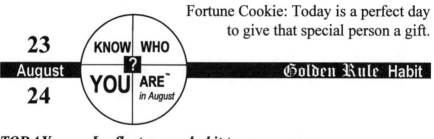

Fortune Cookie: Today is a perfect day to give that special person a gift.

23
August
24

KNOW WHO **?** YOU ARE™ in August

Golden Rule Habit

TODAY... **I reflect on my habit to**
KNOW WHO I AM

My own personal life nemesis has been the need to please others. For me, I should use today's reminder for at least two or three days. This will give me a little more time to remember that my polar star is my character and my conscience – not the good opinion of others.

> *I don't know the key to success*
> *but the key to failure is trying to please everyone.*
> BILL COSBY, AMERICAN COMEDIAN AND ACTOR

> *Character is like the polar star, which keeps its place,*
> *and all stars turn towards it.*
> CONFUCIUS, CHINESE PHILOSOPHER

> *Virtue is the truest nobility.*
> MIGUEL DE CERVANTES, SPANISH AUTHOR

Fortune Cookie: Be assertive when decisive action is needed.

TODAY...   *I reflect on my habit to*
KNOW WHO I AM

Truth and virtue go hand in hand. Of all life's vicissitudes, truth remains unchanged while the rest of life swirls around and in us. If you learn and know your own inspired truth – the rest becomes much easier. When you have learned to practice your truths, life becomes bliss.

Truth is great, and its effectiveness endures.
PTAHHOTEP

There is no greatness
where there is no simplicity, goodness and truth.
LEO TOLSTOY

Fortune Cookie: Treasure what you have.

KNOW WHO **25**
? August
YOU ARE™
in August **26**

𝔊𝔬𝔩𝔡𝔢𝔫 𝔎𝔲𝔩𝔢 Habit

A
U
G

TODAY...   *I reflect on my habit to*
KNOW WHO I AM

Character is what you know you are,
not what others think you are.
MARVA COLLINS AND CIVIA TAMARKIN, AMERICAN EDUCATORS

Son, when a man knows something deep down in his heart...
when he really knows...he doesn't have to argue about it,
doesn't have to prove it. Just knowin', that's enough.
BEN CARTWRIGHT, "BONANZA"

At the day's end, all our footsteps
are added up to see how near.
WILLIAM STANLEY MERWIN, LAST PEOPLE

Fortune Cookie: Good luck is the result of good planning.

TODAY . . . *I reflect on my habit to*
KNOW WHO I AM

Courage is the master of temptation. Courage is the only master that you can count on when you know what is right, and temptation stands there beckoning.

> *Joy and courage make a handsome face.*
> FRENCH PROVERB

> *Life shrinks or expands in proportion to one's courage.*
> ANAIS NIN

> *The secret of happiness is freedom,*
> *and the secret of freedom is courage.*
> LOUIS BRANDEIS, FORMER SUPREME COURT JUSTICE

Fortune Cookie: An exciting opportunity lies ahead if you are not timid.

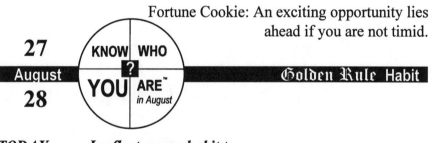

TODAY . . . *I reflect on my habit to*
KNOW WHO I AM

A clear conscience and making memories you can live with later, are both outcomes of a well-lived life.

> *A clear conscience weighs more in the scale*
> *of God and time than an empire.*
> NIKOS KAZANTZAKIS

> *There is only one way to achieve happiness on this terrestrial ball,*
> *and that is to have either a clear conscience or none at all.*
> OGDEN NASH, AMERICAN POET AND HUMORIST, I'M A STRANGER HERE MYSELF

Fortune Cookie:
A small house, well kept, will hold as much happiness as a big one.

TODAY . . .   I reflect on my habit to
KNOW WHO I AM

In the torrent of contemporary living, the concepts of compromise, temptation and virtue can easily become fuzzy. Self reflection, prayer and constant vigilance are the keys to happiness and self-worth. You are all that you have.

Don't compromise yourself. You're all you've got.
JANIS JOPLIN

What you have become is the price you have paid
for what you used to want.
MIGNON MCLAUGHLIN

One's eyes are what one is, one's mouth what one becomes.
JOHN GALSWORTHY, BRITISH AUTHOR, FLOWERING WILDERNESS

Fortune Cookie: You use your creative talents to transform a business environment.

KNOW WHO
?
YOU ARE
in August

29

𝕲𝖔𝖑𝖉𝖊𝖓 𝕽𝖚𝖑𝖊 **Habit**   August

30

TODAY . . .   I reflect on my habit to
KNOW WHO I AM

What lies before us and what lies behind us are small matters compared to what lies within us. And when we bring what is within out into the world, miracles happen.
HENRY DAVID THOREAU

We don't know who we are until we see what we can do.
MARTHA GRIMES

We must all find our true purpose;
like Michalangelo or Mozart or Leonardo da Vinci,
each of us must develop a mission in life.
MICHAEL JACKSON, AMERICAN SINGER

Fortune Cookie: You have a heart of gold.

A
U
G

TODAY... ***I reflect on my habit to***
KNOW WHO I AM

Together we have written the month of August and strengthened our habit of self-reflection and self-understanding. This month we have worked on the fabric of our own lives and the meaning we give to our presence here on earth. What is the gospel according to you?

> *You write a sermon, a chapter each day*
> *By the deeds that you do and the words that you say;*
> *Men read what you write, if it's false or it's true.*
> *Say, what is the gospel according to you?*
> PAUL GILBERT

31
August

KNOW WHO
?
YOU ARE™
in August

I think self-awareness is probably the most important thing towards being a champion.
BILLIE JEAN KING, AMERICAN TENNIS PLAYER

He who is afraid of asking himself questions, is afraid of learning.
DARLENE PATRICK

Great writers leave us not just their works but a way of looking at things.
ELIZABETH JANEWAY

I may be dirty, but I have clean thoughts.
"PIG PEN", PEANUTS COMIC STRIP

Fortune Cookie: You are altruistic and will be involved in many humanitarian projects.

CHAPTER 9

Color "Cue" - Award Gold

"Together We Can Brighten the World We All Share."

180

Give a gift of the *Golden Rule Revolution* to the people in your life.
For quantity pricing see the card at the back of this book. If someone else has used this form, you may
phone: 724-453-0447 e.mail: allofus@icubed.com or visit our website: www.goldenrulerevolution.com

IN SEPTEMBER, REMEMBER TO...
DO YOUR BEST

Kids are going back to school and vacation traffic is winding down. It's time to anchor our resolve to do well, start fresh, and begin again. This month's celebration color is "Award" GOLD. Whenever I see the color "GOLD," I will remember that my life, and what I do with it each day, is important. Whenever I see the color GOLD, I will also remember the GOLDEN RULE.

Let the start of the school year remind you of what teachers over the centuries have always told you, "Do your best!" We've heard it said that "Rome wasn't built in a day." Starting something difficult, or new, is a great time to remember the monuments in Rome. Writing this book, for instance, has been a glorious adventure in joy and in perseverance! It takes lots of patience and overcoming procrastination. Minutes become monuments, one at a time.

Appreciation from others is a great reward for a job well done. There is a definite "force" in powerful words that transfer energy to your mind. Use the words in this GOLDEN RULE REVOLUTION Book, every day, to glean the "force" of inspiration to Do Your Best. To celebrate this important aspect of Golden Rule Living, we will celebrate people down through the centuries who have contributed the best of themselves to us, and to the world we share.

Goal for the month:

Pick a task, even a small one, and give it all you've got!

"Together We Can Brighten the World We All Share."

Somebody said that it couldn't be done,
But he with a chuckle replied,
That 'maybe it couldn't,'
But he would be one
Who wouldn't say so til he tried.

So he buckled right in with the trace of a grin
On his face. If he worried he hid it.
He started to sing
As he tackled the thing
That couldn't be done, and he did it.

EDGAR A. GUEST - "IT COULDN'T BE DONE"

TODAY . . .   ***I practice my habit to***
              DO MY BEST

Aristotle, (384-322 BC) the Greek philosopher, was one of the greatest minds of ancient times. He was a student of Plato, and tutored Alexander the Great in the Macedonian court. His contributions to our philosophical understanding of human existence, set the standard for Western logic and intellectual thinking. He saw that the habits of daily life and not how much you know, are the basis of personal meaning and of excellence.

> *We are what we repeatedly do.*
> *Excellence then, is not an art but a habit.*
> • • •
> *Hope is a waking dream.*
>   ARISTOTLE

Make a habit out of excellence.

𝔊𝔬𝔩𝔡𝔢𝔫 𝔎𝔲𝔩𝔢 Habit   **1**
                                   September
                                   2

TODAY . . .   ***I practice my habit to***
              DO MY BEST

Walt Disney (1901-1966) went bankrupt many times but persevered. In 1928, he developed the cartoon character "Mickey Mouse." During the economic hard times of the 1930's, Disney's cartoons uplifted and brought joy to millions. He was the recipient of 48 Academy Awards. Walt Disney, with hard work and perseverance, made his own dreams come true.

> *Get a good idea and stay with it.*
> *Dog it, and work at it until its done, and done right.*
> • • •
> *All our dreams come true*
> *if we have the courage to pursue them.*
>   WALT DISNEY

Make your stuff into realized dreams of all sizes and shapes.

S
E
P

TODAY . . . ***I practice my habit to***
DO MY BEST

Born in 1925, Margaret Thatcher was the daughter of a grocer. She is the first woman in European history, to have been elected to the office of Prime Minister. She served as Leader of the Conservative Party in Great Britain, between 1979 and 1990. She was a strong advocate of the free market system, and she was the longest serving British Prime Minister of the 20th century.

You may have to fight a battle more than once to win it.

• • •

Pennies do not come from heaven
– they have to be earned right here on earth.

MARGARET THATCHER

Are you a daughter?
What do you need to win your battles?

3 September 4 — do YOUR BEST in September — Golden Rule Habit

TODAY . . . ***I practice my habit to***
DO MY BEST

No matter who you are, if you're seeking inspiration to "Do Your Best," read Booker T. Washington's classic book, *Up From Slavery*. Born as a slave in 1859, Washington grew up to become an advisor to presidents, congressmen and governors. His work toward economic prosperity for blacks led to his role as founder and President of Tuskeegee Institute. His inspiration and wisdom live on today.

The world cares very little about what a man or woman knows; it is what they are determined to do that counts.

• • •

Excellence is to do a common thing in an uncommon way.

BOOKER T. WASHINGTON

Find an area of excellence in your life and praise yourself for it.

TODAY . . .   *I practice my habit to*
DO MY BEST

Agnes Gonxha Bojarhiu was born in Skopje, Yugoslavia in 1910. In 1928, she joined Ireland's Institute of the Blessed Virgin Mary. Soon after, she founded the Order of the Missionaries of Charity in the slums of Calcutta, which now numbers more than 1,000 nuns worldwide. In 1979, her gift of her own life to the poor of the world, earned her the Nobel Peace Prize. Today we know this great woman of the 20th century as Mother Teresa.

> *We can do no great things*
> *– only small things with great love.*
> •   •   •
> *A smile is the beginning of peace.*
> MOTHER TERESA

Do your best in every task, no matter how unimportant it may seem at the time.

Golden Rule Habit

September

5

6

TODAY . . .   *I practice my habit to*
DO MY BEST

The first President of the United States and the commander-in-chief of the colonial armies, George Washington, is known as the father of our country. During the darkest days of his leadership, the winter at Valley Forge, he held our American spirit together with the sheer strength of his character. Commanding the respect of both parties, he was elected our first president in 1789 and re-elected four years later.

> *I hope I shall always possess firmness enough to maintain*
> *what I consider, the most enviable of all titles,*
> *the character of an honest man.*
> GEORGE WASHINGTON

George Washington set the standard of government and of character for all Americans.

S
E
P

186

TODAY... ***I practice my habit to***
DO MY BEST

James Todd Smith lived in a climate of domestic violence in Bay Shore, New York and grew into a violent teenager. Today, as LL Cool J, he's a Grammy-winner, a successful television and film actor and a caring husband and father. *"I finally realized,"* he says, *"Only you can make your life better."*

> *Destructive behavior and a lack of focus will cause you to neglect yourself, your spirit, God and your family. I have learned to focus on my children and loving my family. I can't make sure my family is OK if I'm concentrating on the pain of my own past. I just have to forgive and get on with my life. Now I feel like I'm a winner. I've become the father I always wanted.*
>
> JAMES TODD SMITH, "LL COOL J" - REPRINT FROM USA TODAY - 6/98

7
September
8

Golden Rule Habit

TODAY... ***I practice my habit to***
DO MY BEST

The name of Martin Luther King, Jr. (1929-1968) is synonymous with the cause of freedom. During his life, cut short by an assassin's bullet, he lent the power of his strong personality and eloquent oratory to spearhead the U.S. civil rights movement. In 1964, Congress passed the Civil Rights Act and King became the youngest man ever to receive a Nobel Peace Prize. Like Gandhi, he espoused and practiced non-violence in the pursuit of freedom for his people.

> *We must use time creatively, and forever realize that in time there is always hope to do great things.*
>
> MARTIN LUTHER KING JR.

Martin Luther King, Jr. and John F. Kennedy lived short lives. They stand as proof that great things can be accomplished regardless of our tenure here on earth.

S
E
P

TODAY . . .   *I practice my habit to*
DO MY BEST

Confucius, (China, 551- 479 BC) was one of civilization's most famous teachers. Orphaned at an early age and largely self-educated, he
became the most learned man of his day. He was disturbed deeply by
the human conditions of his time and dedicated his life to social re-
form. His teachings were based on ethics. He taught the radical idea
that the purpose of government was not the pleasure of it's rulers, but
the happiness of it's people.

> *The expectations of life*
> *depend upon diligence;*
> *the mechanic that would perfect his work*
> *must first sharpen his tools.*
> CONFUCIUS

9 September

> *To put the world in the right order,*
> *we must first put the nation in order;*
> *to put the nation in order;*
> *we must first put the family in order;*
> *to put the family in order;*
> *we must first cultivate our personal life;*
> *we must first set our hearts right.*
> CONFUCIUS

S
E
P

Isn't it profound, how true wisdom transcends time?
Words that could have been spoken yesterday here in America,
were in the thoughts of a person who lived 2,500 years ago.

TODAY . . . ***I practice my habit to***
DO MY BEST

Before the age of 2, Helen Adams Keller (1880-1968), was deprived by illness of both her sight and hearing. Helen Keller learned to write, read and speak, and went on to graduate cum laude from Radcliffe College in 1904. In the face of overwhelming disabilities, the courage of Helen Keller shines as a beacon of courage and hope for all of us.

Keep your face to the sunshine and you cannot see the shadows.

• • •

Toleration is the greatest gift of the mind. It requires the same effort of the brain that it takes to balance oneself on a bicycle.

HELEN KELLER

Blindness is an affliction not just limited to the eyes. We all have blind spots in life that interfere with our happiness and with achieving our dreams.

10
September
11

Golden Rule Habit

TODAY . . . ***I practice my habit to***
DO MY BEST

John F. Kennedy, the 35th President of the United States, was assassinated at the age of 46. During his short life, John Kennedy achieved military heroism in WW II, resolved the Cuban Missile Crisis, founded the Peace Corps, backed civil rights, boosted space exploration, established government support for mental health, and defied Soviet attempts to force the Allies out of Berlin.

And so my fellow Americans, ask not what your country can do for you, ask what you can do for your country.

• • •

The time to repair the roof is when the sun is shining.

JOHN FITZGERALD KENNEDY, 35TH PRESIDENT OF THE UNITED STATES

President Kennedy's quotation is an eloquent statement of our times – and our continuing need for the Golden Rule.

TODAY . . .   *I practice my habit to*
   DO MY BEST

Nelson Mandella, (b.1918) former South African President, politician, prisoner and political leader, was the primary force behind the end of South African Apartheid. For the courage of his convictions, he spent more than 25 years of imprisonment for his defiance campaign.

> *Our deepest fear is not that we are inadequate.*
> *Our deepest fear is that we are powerful beyond measure.*
> *It is our light, not our darkness, that most frightens us.*
> *We ask ourselves, 'Who am I to be brilliant, gorgeous,*
> *talented and fabulous? Actually, who are you not to be?'*
> NELSON ROLLHLAHLA MANDELLA

Nelson Mandella speaks at a level of excellence
that few can even imagine.

𝕲𝖔𝖑𝖉𝖊𝖓 𝕽𝖚𝖑𝖊 Habit

do YOUR BEST in September

12
September
13

TODAY . . .   *I practice my habit to*
   DO MY BEST

Born in Prague, Czechoslovakia in 1956, Martina Navratlova defected to the United States after winning the Czech women's singles tennis title in 1975. She dominated women's tennis during the 1980's with an aggressive style based on hours of concentrated practice and preparation for competition. She won Wimbleton nine times (a record), the U.S. Open four times, the Australian Open three times, and the French Open twice.

> *Just go out there and do what you've got to do.*
> MARTINA NAVRATLOVA

Sometimes there is a "grinding it out" quality to doing your best that doesn't come from inspiration or eloquence but from just plain commitment – to accomplish the task and to do it well.

S
E
P

190

TODAY . . . ***I practice my habit to***
DO MY BEST

No matter how you feel about the art of Pablo Picasso, (1881-1973)
his prolific style forever changed our understanding and appreciation
of art. Leader of the School of Paris, he was considered remarkable for
his technical virtuosity and incredible originality. His creative expression evolved through a series of defined "periods" of original artistic
forms, such as cubism and collage.

> *The more technique you have,*
> *the less you have to worry about it.*
>> **PABLO PICASSO**

Working consistently throughout his long lifetime in oil, sculpture,
ceramics and graphic arts, Picasso manifested his personal vision
with industry, diligence and passion.

14 September **15** — **do ★ YOUR BEST** *in September* — **Golden Rule Habit**

TODAY . . . ***I practice my habit to***
DO MY BEST

Dale Carnegie became famous in his own lifetime by bringing out the
best in others. His books of well-phrased rules and the teachings of the
Carnegie Institute for Effective Speaking and Human Relations, have
helped millions. His life is an example of his own message – that success is the result of persistence, patience and personal initiative.

> *The person who goes farthest is generally the one who is willing*
> *to do and dare. The sure-thing boat never gets far from the shore.*
> • • •
> *If you want to gather honey, don't kick over the beehive.*
> • • •
> *When dealing with people, remember that you are not dealing*
> *with creatures of logic, but with creatures of emotion.*
>> **DALE CARNEGIE**

What is your life's message?

TODAY...   *I practice my habit to*
DO MY BEST

Golda Meier (1898-1978) was a founder of the State of Israel and served as its fourth Prime Minister. Born in Russia, she emigrated to Wisconsin where her passion for political activity ignited the Milwaukee Labor Zionist Party. She emigrated to Palestine in 1921 and held key posts before her appointment as Prime Minister in 1969. At her death in 1978, it was revealed that she had suffered from leukemia for 12 years.

You cannot shake hands with a clenched fist.

• • •

Those who do not know how to weep with their whole heart, do not know how to laugh either.

GOLDA MEIER

(Golden Rule Habit

do YOUR BEST *in September*

16
September
17

TODAY...   *I practice my habit to*
DO MY BEST

Abraham Lincoln (1809-1865) preserved the United States of America through its darkest hour, the Civil War. Born in the backwoods of Kentucky and largely self-educated, his life is a symbol of democracy and the ideal of equality. Not a physically handsome man, he was loved and admired for his inner qualities of faithfulness, honesty, resolution, humor and courage.

**S
E
P**

Always bear in mind that your own resolution to succeed is more important than any other thing.

• • •

I do the very best I know how – the very best I can; and I mean to keep on doing so until the end.

• • •

What kills a skunk is the publicity it gives itself.

ABRAHAM LINCOLN

TODAY... ***I practice my habit to***
DO MY BEST

The persistence, faithfulness and ingenuity of Ray A. Kroc, set the stage for the modern fast-food franchising industry. He recognized that the assembly line method of a small McDonald's Brothers hamburger stand in San Bernadino, CA, was simple but efficient. The first McDonald's was opened April 15, 1955. His steadfast devotion to an idea brought financial success, which allowed him to make many charitable contributions to society in his later years.

The quality of an individual is reflected
in the standards they set for themselves.
• • •
It's a matter of having principles.
It's easy to have principles when you're rich.
The important thing is to have principles when you're not.

RAY KROC ·

18
September
19

&olden Rule Habit

TODAY... ***I practice my habit to***
DO MY BEST

The name Gandhi, today stands as a worldwide synonym for courage and peaceful revolution. Mohandas (Mahatma) Gandhi (1869-1948), led the Indian Nationalist movement against British rule, and is esteemed internationally for his doctrine of nonviolence to achieve political and social progress. When once asked for his "message" to the world, he replied, *"My life is my message."* He asserted the unity of mankind under one God, and preached Christian and Muslim ethics along with the Hinduism of his birth.

The only tyrant I accept in this world, is the still voice within.
• • •
A "No," uttered from deep conviction is better and greater than
a "Yes" merely said to please, or worse, to avoid trouble.
• • •
No culture can survive if it attempts to be exclusive. GANDHI

TODAY... *I practice my habit to*
DO MY BEST

Charles de Gaulle rose to world fame as the leader of French resistance. During World War II, his radio appeals broadcast from Britain to the French people to resist and to continue the struggle, earned him a death sentence in absentia. However, his persistence earned him the support of the Allied leaders and he was chosen as president of the provisional government. Later he became the founding President of France's Fifth Republic, which remains in control today.

Nothing great will ever be achieved without great (wo)men,
and (wo)men are great only if they are determined to be so.
• • •
How can one conceive of a one-party system in a country
like France that has over two hundred varieties of cheese?
• • •
Deliberation can be the work of many (wo)men.
Action, of one alone. CHARLES DE GAULLE

Golden Rule Habit | September

20

21

TODAY... *I practice my habit to*
DO MY BEST

The first Polish Pope in Catholic history, John Paul II was the first non Italian in 456 years. Among the usual attributes of greatness, John Paul's fluency in many languages, qualifies him well as an international ambassador for his Church. Despite an assassination attempt in 1981, his passionate commitment to spread the word of God has continued strong throughout his long tenure.

We must strive to multiply bread so that it suffices
for all the tables of mankind.
• • •
To maintain a joyful family requires much from both the
parents and the children. Each member has to become,
in a special way, the servant of all of the others.
JOHN PAUL II

S
E
P

194

TODAY . . .   *I practice my habit to*
DO MY BEST

Andrew Carnegie (1835-1919) embodies the desirable union of entrepreneurial success and civic responsibility. He emigrated from Scotland in 1848 and began work in America as a bobbin boy in a cotton factory. By 1900, Carnegie Steel produced more than a quarter of U.S. steel. Believing that wealth should be used for public good, he retired in 1901 to begin his philanthropic career. He established the Carnegie Endowment for International Peace, the Carnegie Corporation of New York and over 2,800 libraries.

> *Concentration is my motto*
> *– first honesty, then industry, then concentration.*
> • • •
> *The law of competition is best for this race,*
> *because it insures the survival of the fittest.*
>
> ANDREW CARNEGIE

22
September
23

𝔊𝔬𝔩𝔡𝔢𝔫 𝔕𝔲𝔩𝔢 Habit

TODAY . . .   *I practice my habit to*
DO MY BEST

Over the course of his lifetime, Vince Lombardi (1913-1970) became the national symbol for the determination to win. Born in New York City, he played and coached football at Fordham University. In 1959, he became Head Coach of the Green Bay Packers and forged a defeated team into the dominant professional team of the 1960's – winning 5 national NFL championships and the first two Super Bowls.

> *It's not whether you get knocked down, it's whether you get up.*
> • • •
> *The difference between a successful person and others is not a*
> *lack of strength, not a lack of knowledge, but rather a lack of will.*
> • • •
> *The harder you work the harder it is to surrender.*
>
> VINCE LOMBARDI

S
E
P

TODAY . . .   *I practice my habit to*
DO MY BEST

His buoyant faith in God and belief in the power of positive prayer were the groundwork upon which he built a tower of inspiration for the world. Believing that helping people was one of the main tasks of religion, Norman Vincent Peale wrote books and engaged his upbeat oratorical skills, to preach his message to thousands at a time, via mass media. His love, humor and passion made him one of the most popular Protestant ministers in the United States.

When you affirm big, believe big and pray big; big things happen.
• • •
Any fact facing us is not as important as our attitude toward it, for that determines our success or failure.
• • •
Plan your work for today and every day, then work your plan.
NORMAN VINCENT PEALE

Golden Rule Habit

24 September **25**

TODAY . . .   *I practice my habit to*
DO MY BEST

He never held public office, yet Benjamin Franklin (1706-1790) was one of the most famous statesmen of all ages. He is best known for his ingenuity in guiding the separation of the American colonies from Great Britain and for helping to frame the Declaration of Independence. His famous experiment with a kite in a thunderstorm, proved the presence of electricity in lightening.

Diplomacy is the art of helping someone else have your idea.
• • •
The way to see by Faith is to shut the eye of Reason.
• • •
Who is wise? He that learns from everyone.
Who is powerful? He that governs his passions.
Who is rich? He who is content. Who is that? NOBODY.
BENJAMIN FRANKLIN

S
E
P

TODAY...   *I practice my habit to*
DO MY BEST

Susan B(rownell) Anthony, (1820-1906) was the American leader of the women's suffrage movement. She organized the Daughters of Temperance and with Elizabeth Cady Stanton, led the campaign for women's rights laws in New York. The laws guaranteed rights over their children and control of their property and wages. She supported President Lincoln, but opposed suffrage to freedmen without also giving it to women.

Failure is impossible.
SUSAN B. ANTHONY

26
September
27

Golden Rule Habit

TODAY...   *I practice my habit to*
DO MY BEST

Albert Schweitzer (1875-1965) was one of the greatest Christians and missionaries of his time. His life and writing such as "Philosophy of Civilization," exemplified a reverence for nature, that may have been the harbinger of the era of environmentalism. Born in Alsace in Germany, he was a brilliant musician and an authority on the life of Bach. With proceeds from his concerts and lectures Schwietzer built a hospital in Gabon, Africa. Public acknowledgment of his selfless commitment to humanity, won him the Nobel Peace Prize in 1952.

There is no higher religion than human service.
To work for the common good is the greatest creed.
•   •   •
Example is not the main thing in influencing others.
It is the only thing.   ALBERT SCHWEITZER

TODAY . . . *I practice my habit to*
DO MY BEST

Sir Winston Churchill (1874-1965), as a wartime Prime Minister, led Great Britain from the brink of defeat to victory over Hitler's aggression in Europe. He was appointed as Prime Minister in 1939. His refusal to make peace with Hitler, was crucial to maintaining British resistance between 1940 and 1942. He joined Franklin D. Roosevelt and Joseph Stalin, to shape Allied strategy for the war. In 1953, he was knighted and awarded the Nobel Prize in literature.

The price of greatness is responsibility.
• • •
The greatest lesson in life is to know that even fools are right sometimes.
• • •
An appeaser is one who feeds a crocodile, hoping it will eat him last.
SIR WINSTON CHURCHILL

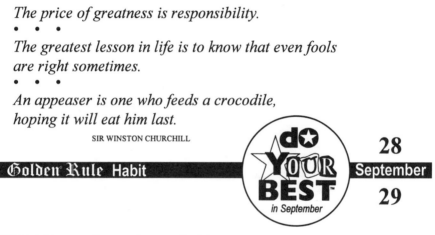

Golden Rule Habit

do YOUR BEST *in September*

28
September
29

TODAY . . . *I practice my habit to*
DO MY BEST

Henry Ford (1863-1947) was an American industrial pioneer and folk hero. His innovations changed forever the economic and social character of America – and the world. His goal was the employment of mass production techniques to make automobiles that were affordable for the average person. He raised pay for his workers above the norm of the day and began a profit sharing plan that distributed up to thirty million dollars a year among his employees. A noted philanthropist, he established the Ford Foundation and the Henry Ford Museum.

A bore is a person who opens his mouth and puts his feats in it.
• • •
My best friend is the person who brings out the best in me.
• • •
Even a mistake may turn out to be the one thing necessary to a worthwhile achievement.   HENRY FORD

S
E
P

198

TODAY . . .   *I practice my habit to*
DO MY BEST

Best known for his contributions to the field of physics, Albert Einstein (1879-1955) was considered by many to have had the greatest mind of all time. Born in Germany, the Nazi government confiscated his property and citizenship because he was Jewish. In 1940, he became an American citizen, holding a post at the Institute for Advanced Studies from 1933 until his death. An ardent pacifist, he received the 1921 Nobel prize in physics.

Try not to become a man/woman of success
but rather try to become a person of value.
• • •
A hundred times a day I remind myself that my life depends on the labors of other people, and that I must exert myself in order to give, in the measure as I have received, and am still receiving.

ALBERT EINSTEIN

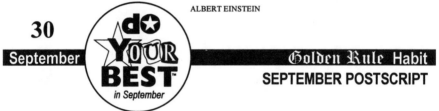

30
September

do YOUR BEST
in September

𝕲𝖔𝖑𝖉𝖊𝖓 𝕽𝖚𝖑𝖊 Habit
SEPTEMBER POSTSCRIPT

S
E
P

In SEPTEMBER and All Year Long...

I will practice my habit to
DO MY BEST.

During this month of September, I featured 30 people from history, who made significant contributions by "Doing Their Best."

Who would you add to the list?

What is your significant contribution?

CHAPTER 10

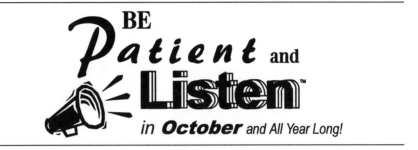

Color "Cue" - Slow-down Lavender

"Together We Can Brighten the World We All Share."

Give a gift of the *Golden Rule Revolution* to the people in your life.
For quantity pricing see the card at the back of this book. If someone else has used this form, you may
phone: 724-453-0447 e.mail: allofus@icubed.com or visit our website: www.goldenrulerevolution.com

IN OCTOBER, REMEMBER TO...
BE PATIENT AND LISTEN

Having known about and lived through the twelve month cycle of the GOLDEN RULE REVOLUTION for ten years now, I welcome October as the month to rest my weary soul. I see peaceful joy in the breathtakingly colorful autumn nature show outside my home and office. I love the sense of calm and quiet appreciation of beauty that I feel under the influence of "Be Patient and Listen."

This month's celebration color is Slow-down LAVENDER. Whenever I see the color LAVENDER, I feel quieter, more tuned to listening, and more connected to those who pass through my day. Think about this especially when you are driving. The increasing statistics about "Road Rage" are a terrible thing. On the road is a time to remember something a friend of mine once said, *"Help everyone that you can, and if you cannot help them, at least don't hurt them."* Drive carefully this month, with caring and respect for others on the road with you.

Enjoy your leisurely stroll (or "scroll") through our inspirations for October. Remember that there is a sparkling spectrum of color in every moment, in every person, and in every autumn leaf. Let the leaves remind you to enjoy the colors of each moment and to appreciate the treasure of "moment jewels" that you will find when you are patient with yourself and listen to your heart.

I've often said that life is like a bag of M&M's. Life is Moments and Memories. October is a month to ask yourself, *"What's the worst that can happen if I don't do...?"* or *"Am I the only person who...?"* or *"How bad can it be...?"*

Goal for the month:

Find the patience to make cherished memories
out of more moments this month.

"Together We Can Brighten the World We All Share."

Slow Dance

AUTHOR UNKNOWN

Have you ever watched kids on a merry-go-round?
Or listened to the rain slapping on the ground?
Ever followed a butterfly's flight
Or gazed at the sun into the fading night?

>   *You better slow down. Don't dance so fast.*
>   *Time is short. The music won't last.*

Do you run through each day – On the fly?
When you ask "How are you?" Do you hear the reply?

When the day is done, do you lie in your bed
With the next hundred chores, running through your head?

>   *You'd better slow down. Don't dance so fast.*
>   *Time is short. The music won't last.*

Ever told your child, we'll do it tomorrow?
And in your haste, not see his sorrow?

Ever lost touch, let a good friendship die,
'Cause you never had time to call and say "Hi"?

>   *You'd better slow down. Don't dance so fast.*
>   *Time is short. The music won't last.*

When you run so fast to get somewhere,
You miss half the fun of getting there.

When you worry and hurry through your day,
It is like an unopened gift...Thrown away.

>   *Life is not a race. Do take it slower.*
>   *Hear the music, before the song is over.*

TODAY...   *I pause for my habit to*
BE PATIENT AND LISTEN

The quality of patience reflects love of self and love of others. Without patience, we miss so much of life while hurrying on to the next thing. Without patience, we miss the beauty of other people.

> *What is this life if, full of care,*
> *We have no time to stop and stare?*
> W.H. DAVIES, "LEISURE" SONGS OF JOY

> *...the unity that binds us all together,*
> *that makes this earth a family, is love.*
> AUTHOR UNKNOWN

Learn to enjoy silence.

Golden Rule Habit   BE *Patient* and **Listen** in October   **1** October **2**

TODAY...   *I pause for my habit to*
BE PATIENT AND LISTEN

The real teachers of patience are our children.

> *You can learn many things from children.*
> *How much patience you have, for instance.*
> FRANKLIN P. JONES

> *Loving a child doesn't mean giving in to all his whims;*
> *to love him/her is to bring out the best in him/her,*
> *to teach him/her to love is what is difficult.*
> NADIA BOULANGER

> *Patience is the ability to count down before you blast off.*
> AUTHOR UNKNOWN

O C T

Our children are 21% of our present and 100% of our future. Be loving and patient.

204

TODAY . . .   *I pause for my habit to*
BE PATIENT AND LISTEN

We know there are people who can chew gum and walk at the same time, but is there anyone who can listen and talk at the same time? Sometimes we don't know when to stop talking.

A closed mouth gathers no feet.
AUTHOR UNKNOWN

You don't learn anything while you're talking.
ALBERT MARKS

You never saw a fish on the wall with it's mouth shut.
SALLY BERGER

A closed mouth gathers no hooks.

3 October **4** — BE *Patient* and **Listen** in October — Golden Rule Habit

TODAY . . .   *I pause for my habit to*
BE PATIENT AND LISTEN

There IS a quiet voice inside of us that is worthy of being listened to. We have named this voice everything from intuition, to conscience, to God – but collectively we all know it is there.

Take a few minutes to listen for the guidance that comes from within your own heart.

O
C
T

In the silence of prayer,
encounter with God is activated.
POPE JOHN PAUL II, "INSEGNAMENTI V", 3, 1138-40

Everything we create in life comes from our inner silence. Give this resource time to bloom. Close your eyes in silence for five minutes.

TODAY . . .   *I pause for my habit to*
BE PATIENT AND LISTEN

I woke up this morning worrying about something I said yesterday. I was kidding around with students in my Caring Habit group at school. I kiddingly used a slang word – and they all gasped that Mrs. Parke had said such a thing. I realized how sensitive kids are and how you create an image with them that is very fragile. Then I realized that for me, this was a time for a prayer.

> *Any concern too small to be turned into a prayer,*
> *is too small to be made into a burden.*
> CORRIE TEN BOOM, CLIPPINGS FROM MY NOTEBOOK

Feel the lightness of turning every burden
and worry into a prayer.

Golden Rule Habit

BE
Patient
and
Listen
in October

5
October
6

TODAY . . .   *I pause for my habit to*
BE PATIENT AND LISTEN

Have you heard of "road rage" and other terms that describe the way we too often treat each other? The GOLDEN RULE REVOLUTION will help each of us remember to be more respectful and considerate, as we go through a normal day. Improving our own sense of humor will also help.

> *Today's society will ignore*
> *almost any form of rudeness except,*
> *getting in the express line with two extra items.*
> PAUL SWEENEY

O
C
T

We are funny.
Laugh at human nature and feel the peace it brings forth in you.

TODAY . . . **I pause for my habit to**
BE PATIENT AND LISTEN

"Hi, How are ya?"
"How's it going?"
"What's happening?"

Do you really mean it?
Do you want an answer?
Do you have time to listen to the answer?
What do you do when someone really shares with you,
a problem or a burden they are carrying?

There is no greater gift than a sympathetic ear.
FRANK TYGER

Today, ask someone how they are doing
and then really listen to their answer.

7
October
8

BE
Patient
and
Listen
in October

Golden Rule Habit

TODAY . . . **I pause for my habit to**
BE PATIENT AND LISTEN

The Golden Rule is all about mutual respect. Respect for another person is best and truest when it comes from the heart. Sometimes, however, a structure of behavior involving manners, can help bridge that awkward period in a new relationship or tide you over when you don't know what else to do.

The great secret is not having bad manners
or good manners or any other particular sort of manners,
but having the same manners for all human souls.
GEORGE BERNARD SHAW, BRITISH PLAYWRIGHT

Manners are an expression of respect.

TODAY...   *I pause for my habit to*
BE PATIENT AND LISTEN

Television has changed the course of human history. It has turned us into a "sound-byte" generation who finds it difficult to pay attention for more than 30 seconds. It has also interfered with our sense of discrimination about use of time. Too often, *"What's on TV?"* is the plan for our evening. Pay attention this month, to your use of time. Be patient enough to plan alternative activities with your family and friends instead of watching TV.

> *There was an educational channel in the good old days*
> *– it was called "OFF."*
> AUTHOR UNKNOWN

Watch the TV channel "OFF" this month.

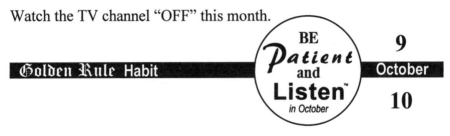

9

ⓖⓞⓛⓓⓔⓝ ⓡⓤⓛⓔ Habit   October

10

TODAY...   *I pause for my habit to*
BE PATIENT AND LISTEN

There's an old adage, *"If you don't have time to do it right, do you have time to do it again?"* Take time today to be thorough in your evaluation of alternatives. Find out more about your choices and determine a path based on complete understanding.

> *Be patient with life.*
> *Sometimes the road less traveled*
> *is less traveled for a reason.*
> JERRY SEINFELD, "SEINFELD"

Have you ever been saved from disaster because
something didn't happen fast enough?

O
C
T

208

TODAY ...   *I pause for my habit to*
BE PATIENT AND LISTEN

Our "instant gratification" life is a fertile ground for placing too much value on the gratification that comes the soonest or feels the best right now. Spend some time this month – taking a long range look at your short term choices. Sometimes you just want to get back at so-and-so – or get angry because someone seemed to let you down. Is your action a *"Much more than"* or a *"How I feel right this minute"*?

> *Life is much more than how you feel right this minute.*
> ELAINE PARKE

When this moment is hard to bear...
remember that the continuity of living is made sweet
by the variety of its landscapes; past, present, and future.

11
October

12

BE
Patient
and
Listen™
in October

𝔊𝔬𝔩𝔡𝔢𝔫 ℜ𝔲𝔩𝔢 Habit

TODAY ...   *I pause for my habit to*
BE PATIENT AND LISTEN

There are many stories of great people down through the centuries, who have won by practicing patience. Firm patience is one of the essential qualities of non-violent change. Ghandi changed India with non-violence because he believed in a dynamic called "Satyagraha." It is a force that works silently and slowly. In reality, Ghandi believed that no other force in the world is so direct or so strong.

> *In any contest between power and patience,*
> *bet on patience.*
> W.B. PRESCOTT

Remember Ghandi.

TODAY ... *I pause for my habit to*
BE PATIENT AND LISTEN

Patience is power. Many times, a little patience pays off. I remember moving to a new city with several job opportunities – one a great job and the other so-so. I wanted the better job, but didn't hear from the company for a long time after the interview. Each day that I waited, I was tempted to call and accept the other offer. Then, nearly two weeks later, the call came and the better job was mine.

He that can have patience can have what he will.
BENJAMIN FRANKLIN, AMERICAN PATRIOT, WRITER AND INVENTOR

Patience is power; with time and patience
the mulberry leaf becomes silk.
CHINESE PROVERB

Patience is the companion of wisdom.
ST. AUGUSTINE

Practice quiet wisdom.

BE
Patient
and
Listen
in October

13
October
14

Golden Rule Habit

TODAY ... *I pause for my habit to*
BE PATIENT AND LISTEN

Raising children teaches us patience in many ways. One of the challenges is to resist "doing it for them" because (whatever "it" is) we can do it faster and better. Children who are not allowed to struggle with new challenges will not know how to be self-reliant adults.

When you give someone a fish,
you feed them for a day.
When you teach someone to fish,
you've fed them for a lifetime.
OLD PROVERB

O
C
T

As a parent, how difficult this is to do. Without reaching for the shoestrings, patiently encourage a small child to tie his/her own shoe from beginning to end.

TODAY...   *I pause for my habit to*
BE PATIENT AND LISTEN

Breaking up a "daunting" task into smaller pieces makes all the difference. Writing this book, for me, is a great example of that. As a former advertising executive, I wrote "sound-byte" length copy all my life. I'm sure I have written many book-lengths of it – but never added it up. When I decided to write this book, the task seemed impossible. I thought I could never write 200 or 300 pages all at once. I treated each day as one sound-byte of writing – day by day, and sooner than I thought – the book was done.

> *Life is a trial, mile by mile, life is hard, yard by yard;*
> *but life is a cinch, inch by inch.*
> OLD ENGLISH SAYING

The inches of life are it's moments.

15
October
16

BE **Patient** and **Listen**
in October

(Golden Rule Habit)

TODAY...   *I pause for my habit to*
BE PATIENT AND LISTEN

Imagine what a bridge or a building would look like if the builders never took time to plan first and just started building? When you take time, and are patient enough to plan, there's room for creativity to come to light. When you feel hurried or too rushed to be patient, ask yourself, is the rush, or is the quality of the solution, more important?

> *No matter what difficulty you're facing,*
> *the practice of creative patience*
> *is a proven road to solutions.*
> REV. NORMAN VINCENT PEALE, AMERICAN CLERGYMAN AND AUTHOR

O
C
T

We have 1,440 minutes each day to patiently listen
for the voice from within our own hearts.

TODAY . . .   *I pause for my habit to*
BE PATIENT AND LISTEN

Both take patience – but there is a difference between anticipation and anxious worry while we wait. If you find yourself worrying about something in the future, an operation, or even a deadline you have to meet for a project, try to think of the positive outcomes and define tasks you can do while waiting. This may improve the outcome.

Steady, patient, persevering thinking, will generally surmount every obstacle in the search after truth.
EMMOMS

Be patient with everyone, but above all, with yourself.
ST. FRANCIS DE SALES

Is patience with yourself, the most difficult for you?

𝕲𝖔𝖑𝖉𝖊𝖓 𝕽𝖚𝖑𝖊 Habit

BE
Patient
and
Listen™
in October

17
October
18

TODAY . . .   *I pause for my habit to*
BE PATIENT AND LISTEN

I wanted to find a quote from Thomas Edison about this subject. Most of us know the story of how he tried 1,000 ways to make a light bulb before he was successful. His effort is proof of the fact that the really valuable achievements in life do not come easily. The real secret to success is simply, have patience, stick with it and don't quit.

Genius begins great works; labor alone finishes them.
JOSEPH JOUBERT

If I have ever made any valuable discoveries,
it has been owing more to patient attention,
than to any other talent.
SIR ISAAC NEWTON, BRITISH MATHEMATICIAN

We fool ourselves when we allow failure to rein over perseverance.

O
C
T

TODAY . . .   *I pause for my habit to*
BE PATIENT AND LISTEN

I'm a terrible "waiter." I've found that the best way to handle it is not to wait at all. This doesn't mean to move up the date of what you are waiting for – but to refuse to adopt a "waiting" frame of mind. Every moment has its own treasures. When we are "waiting" they are lost. Spend your moments in a "treasure-finding" instead of a "waiting" frame of mind.

> *All things come round to him who will but wait.*
> HENRY WADSWORTH LONGFELLOW, AMERICAN POET

> *Anticipating is even more fun than recollecting.*
> MALCOLM S. FORBES, SR., AMERICAN BUSINESSMAN

When I feel impatient, I remember Christmas morning AFTER the presents are unwrapped.

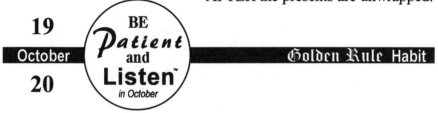

19
October
20

BE *Patient* and **Listen** in October

𝔊𝔬𝔩𝔡𝔢𝔫 ℜ𝔲𝔩𝔢 Habit

TODAY . . .   *I pause for my habit to*
BE PATIENT AND LISTEN

Why do we always expect people to be logical? How often have you found yourself saying, *"I don't see why he/she did that,"* or *"That made no sense,"* or *"What did he/she do THAT for?"* People are meant to be loved and cared about from the heart, not the mind. So often, there is more to the story than we can see from our perspective. Be patient and forgiving with others, especially children.

> *When you handle yourself, use your head;*
> *when you handle others, use your heart.*
> DONNA REED, "THE DONNA REED SHOW"

How easy to say and how difficult to do – especially as a parent.

TODAY . . . **I pause for my habit to
BE PATIENT AND LISTEN**

When we have patience, the future doesn't stop changing our lives just because we've grown up.

> *To endure is the first thing a child ought to learn,*
> *and that which he will have the most need to know.*
> JEAN JACQUES ROUSSEAU

> *There is always one moment in childhood*
> *when the door opens and lets the future in.*
> GRAHAM GREENE, THE POWER AND THE GLORY

The future is entering every one of our
1,440 minutes each day.

𝕲𝖔𝖑𝖉𝖊𝖓 𝕽𝖚𝖑𝖊 Habit

BE
Patient
and
Listen
in October

21
October

22

TODAY . . . **I pause for my habit to
BE PATIENT AND LISTEN**

Think about how many stress-reduction, sleeping aid and digestion products are sold each day. Ask yourself WHY.

> *Patience can be bitter, but it's fruit is sweet.*
> ROSSEAU

> *Unquiet meals make ill digestions.*
> *How poor are they that have not patience!*
> WILLIAM SHAKESPEARE, BRITISH PLAYWRIGHT AND POET

O
C
T

Remember, Shakespeare never took a TUMS or
read a Stress Reduction pamphlet.

TODAY...   *I pause for my habit to*
BE PATIENT AND LISTEN

Children learn by example and we are known by our examples. People who teach us how to influence others say that we deliver only 9% of our message with words and the rest with our gestures and our actions. Teaching patience by example is the best way to influence our children. In the car, do your children see you as patient and caring with other drivers on the road?

> *There is no such thing as preaching patience into people,*
> *unless you make the sermon so long*
> *they have to practice while they listen.*
> HENRY WARD BEECHER

I hope this "sermon" for October isn't too long.

TODAY...   *I pause for my habit to*
BE PATIENT AND LISTEN

In life, when you don't succeed the first time you try something,
You don't just throw up your hands and say it can't be done.
Being a good student is hard work, takes patience, and sticking to it.
WARD CLEAVER, "LEAVE IT TO BEAVER"

> *Be not afraid of growing slowly,*
> *be afraid only of standing still.*
> CHINESE PROVERB

> *The key to everything is patience. You only get the chicken*
> *alive by hatching the egg, not by smashing it.*
> ARNOLD H. GLASOW

TODAY...   *I pause for my habit to*
BE PATIENT AND LISTEN

It takes patience to be a friend.

The most called-upon prerequisite of a friend is an accessible ear.
MAYA ANGELOU, AMERICAN POET, THE HEART OF A WOMAN

You never really understand a person
until you consider things from his point of view.
HARPER LEE, AMERICAN AUTHOR, TO KILL A MOCKINGBIRD

You have 1,440 minutes today.
Make time to fully understand and listen to others.

Golden Rule Habit   BE *Patient* and **Listen** *in October*   **25** October **26**

TODAY...   *I pause for my habit to*
BE PATIENT AND LISTEN

Make this a quiet day where the world comes in to your heart with beauty and grace. Enjoy the simplicity of today.

Remember the forgotten shreds of simplicity
in our quiet hearts.
AUTHOR UNKNOWN

Adopt the pace of nature: her secret is patience.
RALPH WALDO EMERSON

Slow down, simplify and be kind.
NAOMI JUDD, AMERICAN COUNTRY SINGER

Thank you Naomi, your thought puts it all together.

OCT

TODAY . . .   *I pause for my habit to*
BE PATIENT AND LISTEN

Sometimes I find myself being impatient with others. I really notice this when someone says to me, *"Haven't you finished that report or cleaned the kitchen yet, etc."* I always know why it isn't done. My own reasons are justifiable reasons. So are someone else's.

> *Waiting in a hurry*
> *– the definition of Impatience.*
> AUTHOR UNKNOWN

> *It's easy finding reasons why other folks should be patient.*
> GEORGE ELIOT, BRITISH AUTHOR

...especially at work when you are writing a report.

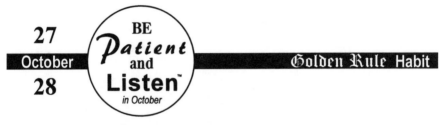

27 October **28**   BE *Patient* and **Listen**™ *in October*   𝔊𝔬𝔩𝔡𝔢𝔫 ℜ𝔲𝔩𝔢 Habit

TODAY . . .   *I pause for my habit to*
BE PATIENT AND LISTEN

According to Drucker, communications is 7% words and 93% everything else. We forget this when we can't wait to get our own opinion or story or point of view across in a conversation.

> *If you are quiet, you may hear a compliment.*
> CHANELLE, AGE 12

> *The most important thing in communication is to hear what isn't being said.*
> PETER F. DRUCKER

O C T

Make today a "practice listening" day.

TODAY...   *I pause for my habit to*
BE PATIENT AND LISTEN

Patience is a key factor in avoiding many of the problems we have in life. How many road accidents wouldn't have happened if people weren't in such a hurry? How many arguments would be avoided if we waited and really thought about the point of view of another person?

> *When angry, count ten before you speak;*
> *if very angry, count to a hundred.*
>
> THOMAS JEFFERSON, THIRD PRESIDENT OF THE UNITED STATES

When you get to the end of your rope, tie a knot, hang on, and swing!
LEO BUSCAGLIA

Our October inspirations wouldn't be complete without counting to ten. Swinging and enjoying the end of your rope is a pretty great thought too. Try it!

Golden Rule Habit   BE *Patient* and **Listen** in October   **29** October **30**

TODAY...   *I pause for my habit to*
BE PATIENT AND LISTEN

Patience is a key to happiness. It is the difference between "feeling out of control" in your life, and feeling as though all things are happening in perfect order. Accepting that we don't understand everything – but trusting in the butterfly – can bring happiness to moments that otherwise would be rushed into nothingness.

> *Happiness is like a butterfly.*
> *The more you chase it, the more it will elude you.*
> *But, if you turn your attention to other things,*
> *it comes and softly sits on your shoulder.*
>
> VIKTOR FRANKL, HOLOCAUST SURVIVOR & PHILOSOPHER

O
C
T

Sit and watch a butterfly, if only in your imagination.

TODAY . . .   ***I pause for my habit to***
BE PATIENT AND LISTEN

When I was just 19, I read this passage from *Letters to a Young Poet*.
Since then, it has been an anchor of perspective for my life journey

> *Have patience with everything unresolved in your heart*
> *and try to love the questions themselves as if they were*
> *glorious books of mystery. Don't search for the answers,*
> *which could not be given to you now, because you would not*
> *be able to live them. And the point is to live everything.*
> *Live the questions now. Perhaps then, someday far*
> *into the future, you will gradually, without even noticing it,*
> *live your way into the answer.*
>
> RAINER MARIA REILKE, GERMAN POET AND PHILOSOPHER

31
October

Still achieving,
still pursuing,
learn to labor
and to wait.

HENRY WADSWORTH LONGFELLOW

Endurance is patience concentrated.

THOMAS CARLYLE

Our patience will achieve more than our force.

EDMUND BURKE

O
C
T

Remember the forgotten shreads of simplicity
in our quiet hearts.

AUTHOR UNKNOWN

As we leave October, let Reilke's letter to a young poet
anchor our journey together.

CHAPTER 11

Color "Cue" - Sunny Yellow

"Together We Can Brighten the World We All Share."

Give a gift of the *Golden Rule Revolution* to the people in your life.
For quantity pricing see the card at the back of this book. If someone else has used this form, you may
phone: 724-453-0447 e.mail: allofus@icubed.com or visit our website: www.goldenrulerevolution.com

IN NOVEMBER, REMEMBER TO...
SHOW A POSITIVE ATTITUDE

This is my favorite month's habit – To Show a Positive Attitude. Our celebration color is "SUNNY Yellow." Yellow is cheerful – the radiance of the day's new sun as it first rises into the morning sky. This is the month to work on our perspective about life and to share a positive attitude more often. Sometimes it is necessary to "fake it 'til we make it." When we do this, we often find that a "true" positive attitude will come about more quickly. Meanwhile, we've curtailed our negative ripples from spreading out to other family members, friends, and co-workers. Enjoy the moments as they happen this month, especially the joy of sharing the Thanksgiving holiday with friends and family. Make positive memories to savor again and again.

Over the years, from friends and the internet, I've collected many short jokes or humorous children's comments. This month, to "Show a Positive Attitude," I am sharing one each day with you. If you have some good positive attitude "one-liners," please share them with me.

Goal for the month:

On every excursion, wear JOY in your smile.

"Together We Can Brighten the World We All Share."

Attitude

CHARLES SWINDOLL

The longer I live,
the more I realize the impact of attitude on life.

Attitude, to me, is more important than facts.

It is more important than the past, than education,
than money, than circumstances, than failures,
than successes, than what other people think or say or do.
It is more important than appearance, giftedness or skill.

It will make or break a company... a church ...a home.

The remarkable thing is, we have a choice everyday,
regarding the attitude we will embrace for that day.

We cannot change the inevitable.

The only thing we can do is play on the one string we have,
and that is our attitude.

I am convinced that life is 10% what happens to me
and 90% how I react to it.

And so it is with you...
we are in charge of our Attitudes.

TODAY . . . **I find JOY in my habit to**
SHOW A POSITIVE ATTITUDE

Humor is a great "sunshine maker." Nothing lightens us up more than a good laugh or even just a quiet chuckle. A fourth-grade teacher gave her students the first phrase of a list of famous sayings and asked them to provide original endings. You will find some of these, plus a few other jewels of humor at the end of each daily inspiration.

> *Lighten up this week. A laugh at your*
> *own expense costs you nothing.*
> AUTHOR UNKNOWN

If you want to be gloomy, there's gloom enough to keep you glum;
if you want to be happy, there's gleam enough to keep you glad.
MALTHIE D. BABCOCK

The grass is always greener when you
— *remember to water it.*

Golden Rule Habit Show a P☺sitive ATTITUDE in November **1** November **2**

TODAY . . . **I find JOY in my habit to**
SHOW A POSITIVE ATTITUDE

I hope you took a moment to read the paragraph on attitude by Charles Swindoll at the beginning of this November section of your GOLDEN RULE REVOLUTION. Read it every day and use its wisdom to anchor your perspective and your attitude for that day. Growth, beauty, and joy can only appear in your life when you provide the positive attitude climate.

> *Life is too good to feel bad.*
> MOTRIN - TV ADVERTISING COMMERCIAL

Onions make people cry but we've not yet discovered
a vegetable that makes people laugh.
WILL ROGERS

Always have good thoughts — *they may break into words at any time.*

N
O
V

TODAY . . . I find JOY in my habit to
SHOW A POSITIVE ATTITUDE

Smiles improve our attitudes and make life easier. Smiling stimulates the nervous system to produce "cerebral morphine." This hormone gives us a pleasant feeling and has an anesthetic effect. Smiles use less energy than frowns. It takes 72 muscles to frown and only 14 to smile.

When you're feeling "down," you can help lift your spirits with a smile. Call or plan to see a friend who is outgoing and upbeat. Find a comedy channel on your TV or even find a "smiling" website. Here's one I found. Website – http://members.aol.com/bunnybeat/smiley.html

Start every day off with a smile – and get it over with.
W.C. FIELDS, AMERICAN ACTOR

Smile! It improves your face value.
"ZIGGY", TOM WILSON

Love makes the world go round but — *laughter keeps us from falling off.*

3 November 4 — Show a Positive ATTITUDE™ in November — Golden Rule Habit

TODAY . . . I find JOY in my habit to
SHOW A POSITIVE ATTITUDE

Keeping a positive outlook in the face of adversity, is easier said than done. This is where our faith communities can be helpful.

If your efforts are sometimes greeted with indifference, don't lose heart – the sun puts on a great show every daybreak, yet most of the people in the audience go on sleeping.
ARDNA F. TEIXERIA

'Tis easy enough to be pleasant, when life flows along like a song. But the man worthwhile is smiling, when everything else goes dead wrong. ELLA WHEELER WILCOX

Cheer up: Birds have bills too, but they keep on singing.
"ZIGGY," TOM WILSON

It's better to light one candle — *than to waste electricity.*

TODAY . . . *I find JOY in my habit to*
SHOW A POSITIVE ATTITUDE

Are you concerned about how people treat one another – especially in public – like when shopping, or sightseeing? When you start to think there's no civility left in public places, just remember that you can actually help shift attitudes around you with the influence of your own attitude. There are people who make cheering up others their mission. It's a great idea and a great way to make life better for ourselves.

> *If all the good people were clever,*
> *And all clever people were good.*
> *The world would be nicer than ever*
> *We thought that it possibly could.*
> ELIZABETH WORDSWORTH, "THE CLEVER AND THE GOOD"

The shortest distance between two people
— *is paved with smiles and laughter.*

Golden Rule Habit — Show a P☺sitive ATTITUDE in November — November 5 6

TODAY . . . *I find JOY in my habit to*
SHOW A POSITIVE ATTITUDE

I've heard it said that "balance is everything." Even though a positive attitude makes life so much easier – there is merit to the idea that some of life's low spots, help us appreciate and cherish life's joys.

> *My great hope is to laugh as much as I cry;*
> *to get my work done and try to love somebody*
> *and have the courage to accept the love in return.*
> MAYA ANGELOU, AMERICAN POET

What the world really needs is more love and less paperwork.
PEARL BAILEY, AMERICAN SINGER-ACTRESS

All sunshine makes a desert.
ARAB PROVERB

N O V

TODAY . . .   *I find JOY in my habit to*
SHOW A POSITIVE ATTITUDE

Showing a positive attitude includes what you "don't," as well as what you do. The worst offender in the attitude department is unkind gossip.

> *If you are tempted to reveal,*
> *A tale someone has told to you*
> *About another, Before you speak,*
>> *Make it pass three gates of gold:*
>> *First, 'Is it true?' Then, 'Is it needful?'*
>> *And then, 'Is it kind?'*
> *And if to reach your lips at last*
> *It passes through these gateways three,*
>> *Then you may tell the tale, nor fear*
>> *What the result of speech may be.*
>>
>> BETH DAY

Better to light a candle than
— to light a stick of dynamite.

7

November

8

(𝔊𝔬𝔩𝔡𝔢𝔫 ℜ𝔲𝔩𝔢 Habit)

TODAY . . .   *I find JOY in my habit to*
SHOW A POSITIVE ATTITUDE

Victor Frankel survived the Nazi concentration camps and wrote a book entitled, *Man's Search for Meaning*. I will always remember the distinction he made between the words, Liberty and Freedom. *"Liberty,"* he said, *"is the condition of being free from restriction, confinement, servitude or forced labor. Freedom is the capacity to exercise choice and the right to act, believe, or express oneself, in the manner of one's own choosing."*

> *No one can make you unhappy without your consent.*
> AUTHOR UNKNOWN

> *It isn't your position that makes you happy or unhappy;*
> *it's your disposition.*
> AUTHOR UNKNOWN

I've learned that even when I have pain — *I don't have to be one.*

TODAY . . .   I find JOY in my habit to
SHOW A POSITIVE ATTITUDE

According to Dr. Annette Goodheart at website www.teehee.com
– laughter is not only good for your attitude it:
>*Strengthens your immune system,*
>*Enhances your cardiovascular flexibility,*
>*Increases your spirit quotient,*
>*Helps you think more clearly,*
>*Puts a twinkle in your eye,*
>*Increases your information retention,*
>*Replenishes your creative juices,*
>*Pops you out of emotional ruts,*
>*Enhances perspective and reminds you of the bigger picture,*
>*Releases and transforms emotional pain and*
>*Enriches your deeper connection with other people.*

Never trust a dog to — *watch your food.*

Show a P☺sitive ATTITUDE in November

𝕲𝖔𝖑𝖉𝖊𝖓 𝕽𝖚𝖑𝖊 Habit   November

9

10

TODAY . . .   I find JOY in my habit to
SHOW A POSITIVE ATTITUDE

Love is only four letters but its meanings fill volumes.One synonym for love is the word acceptance. There is also a peacefulness about the idea of acceptance that helps keep a positive attitude. Today, think about how you accept the weaknesses and annoying habits of others.

Rainbows are the apology of angry skies.
SYLVIA A. VOIROL

Life teaches us to be less harsh with ourselves and with others.
JOHANN WOLFGANG VON GOETHE, GERMAN PLAYWRIGHT

N O V

Don't count your chickens — *it takes too long.*

TODAY . . .   *I find JOY in my habit to*
SHOW A POSITIVE ATTITUDE

The problem is not the problem.
The problem is one's attitude about the problem
JEFFREY A. TIMMONS

Joy is not in things; it is in us.
RICHARD WAGNER

The excursion is the same when you go looking for your sorrow,
as when you go looking for your joy.
EUDORA WELTY, "THE WIDE NET"

The only time the world beats a path to your door
— is when you're in the bathroom.

11
November

12

Show a P☺sitive ATTITUDE in November

𝕲𝖔𝖑𝖉𝖊𝖓 𝕽𝖚𝖑𝖊 Habit

TODAY . . .   *I find JOY in my habit to*
SHOW A POSITIVE ATTITUDE

Enjoying the present moment and looking ahead to the future is an important key to a positive attitude. Practice this today. What is beautiful around you right now? What moments are planned today where you will find joy or fulfillment? Are you going to see an old friend, work on a project with a co-worker, or walk in the park?

Keep your face to the sunshine, and you'll never see the shadows.
DEBBYE TURNER, MISS AMERICA 1990

Nobody gets to live life backward.
Look ahead – that's where your future lies.
ANN LANDERS, ADVICE COLUMNIST

It's a long old road, but I know I'm gonna find the end.
BESSIE SMITH, AMERICAN GOSPEL SINGER

Never put off 'til tomorrow — *what you should have done yesterday.*

N
O
V

TODAY... I find JOY in my habit to
SHOW A POSITIVE ATTITUDE

A Recipe for the Blues
Here's a recipe for the blues which is worth a dozen medical remedies:

Take one spoonful of pleasant memories.
Take two spoonfuls of endeavors for the happiness of others.
Take two spoonfuls of forgetfulness of sorrow.
Mix well with a half pint of cheerfulness.
Take a portion of this mixture every hour of the day.
FRANCES WILLARD

Lead me not into temptation — *I can find the way myself.*

Never knock on death's door — *ring the doorbell and run.*
(he hates that!)

𝕲𝖔𝖑𝖉𝖊𝖓 𝕽𝖚𝖑𝖊 Habit — Show a P☺sitive ATTITUDE in November — **13** November **14**

TODAY... I find JOY in my habit to
SHOW A POSITIVE ATTITUDE

Being able to laugh at ourselves is a great way to avoid self-importance. I only found 3 quotes about laughing at yourself – and they're worth a few laughs! If you find some quotes in your own travels, please send them to me. Seeing humor in our own actions is a great form of self-acceptance and a terrific way to "lighten up"

Blessed are they who can laugh at themselves,
for they shall never cease to be amused.
AUTHOR UNKNOWN

You grow up the day you have your first real laugh at yourself.
ETHEL BARRYMORE

Laugh at yourself first, before anyone else can.
ELSA MAXWELL

It's not hard to meet expenses — *they're everywhere.*

N O V

230

TODAY . . . **I find JOY in my habit to**
SHOW A POSITIVE ATTITUDE

Maintaining a positive attitude during adversity is easier when we remember that we actually do "get through" most tough set-backs. Quite
often, something better happens. Many people have lost their jobs, for
instance, and found a new lease on life and a new direction that they
never would have taken otherwise.

> *The soul would have no rainbow had the eyes no tears.*
> JOHN VANCE CHENEY

The worst thing in your life may contain seeds of the best.
When you can see crisis as an opportunity,
your life becomes not easier, but more satisfying.
JOE KOGEL

When you're living on the edge –
be sure you're wearing your seat belt.

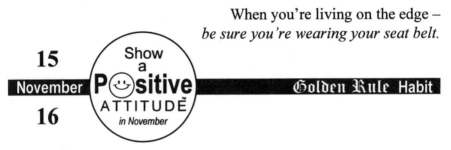

15
November

16

Show a P😊sitive ATTITUDE in November

𝔊𝔬𝔩𝔡𝔢𝔫 𝔙𝔲𝔩𝔢 Habit

TODAY . . . **I find JOY in my habit to**
SHOW A POSITIVE ATTITUDE

Today's positive attitude "thought" – that a smile enhances appearance more than cosmetics or accessories – could cause a drop in sales
for the cosmetics and clothing industry. Of course, just when we thought
they couldn't possibly figure out how to sell us something to make a
smile more beautiful – the teeth whiteners came on the market!

There is no cosmetic for beauty like happiness. LADY MARGUREITE BLESSINGTON

Making joy in life is a woman's best cosmetic. ROSALIND RUSSELL

A winning smile is the best accessory any dress ever had. C. TERRY CLINE,JR.

You're never fully dressed without a smile. MARTIN CHARNIN, ANNIE

N
O
V

If God had wanted me to touch my toes
— *he would have put them on my knees.*

TODAY . . .   I find JOY in my habit to
SHOW A POSITIVE ATTITUDE

There are "last ditch effort" situations when a firm and even angry attitude seems to be necessary to get what you need. HOWEVER, many people have gotten into the habit of using anger and intimidation all the time. We learned from Mary Poppins that "a spoonful of sugar makes the medicine go down."

You can catch more flies with honey than vinegar.
AUTHOR UNKNOWN

Sandwich every piece of criticism between two layers of praise.
MARY KAY ASH

It's nice to work with friendly people. Be one.
AUTHOR UNKNOWN

For every action there is an
— equal and opposite criticism.

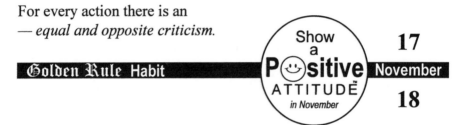

Golden Rule Habit — Show a Positive Attitude in November — 17 November 18

TODAY . . .   I find JOY in my habit to
SHOW A POSITIVE ATTITUDE

If there is any other word that is a synonym for "positive attitude" it is the word "hope." Each is impossible without the other.

Hope is the only good that is common to all (wo)men;
those who have nothing else possess hope still.
THALES

Hope springs eternal in the human breast.
ALEXANDER POPE, BRITISH POET

Where there is life there is hope.
CICERO

He who loses hope may then part with anything.
WILLIAM CONGREVE, BRITISH AUTHOR AND PLAYWRIGHT

The hardness of the butter — *is proportional to the softness of the bread.*

N
O
V

TODAY . . . *I find JOY in my habit to*
SHOW A POSITIVE ATTITUDE

Many have found inspiration in The Optimist Creed. It has been used to help patients recover from illness or to motivate the players on sports teams. Optimist International adopted this creed in 1922. It was originally published in 1912, in a book by Christian D. Larson, who believed that people have powers which can be successfully mobilized, with the proper attitude.

The Optimist Creed

OPTIMIST INTERNATIONAL® COPYRIGHT © 1999

Promise Yourself —

To be so strong that nothing can disturb your peace of mind.

*To talk health, happiness and prosperity
to every person you meet.*

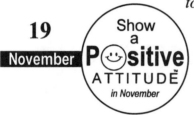

*To make all your friends feel
that there is something in them.*

*To look at the sunny side of
everything and make your optimism
come true.*

*To think only of the best, to work only for the best and
to expect only the best.*

*To be just as enthusiastic about the success of others
as you are about your own.*

*To forget the mistakes of the past and press on
to the greater achievements of the future.*

*To wear a cheerful countenance at all times and
give every living creature you meet a smile.*

*To give so much time to the improvement of yourself
that you have no time to criticize others.*

*To be too large for worry, too noble for anger, too strong for fear,
and too happy to permit the presence of trouble.*

A penny saved — *is not much.*

TODAY . . . **I find JOY in my habit to**
SHOW A POSITIVE ATTITUDE

You have to sniff out joy.
Keep your nose to the joy-trail.
BUFFY SAINTE-MARIE, NATIVE AMERICAN FOLK SINGER

Aqua-dexterous (adjective) – possessing the ability
to turn the bathtub on and off with your toes.
AUTHOR UNKNOWN

Early to bed and early to rise — *is first in the bathroom.*

A bird in the hand — *is a real mess.*

𝔊𝔬𝔩𝔡𝔢𝔫 𝔑𝔲𝔩𝔢 Habit | Show a P☺sitive ATTITUDE in November | **20** November **21**

TODAY . . . **I find JOY in my habit to**
SHOW A POSITIVE ATTITUDE

One Hug – The Universal Rx
AUTHOR UNKNOWN

No moving parts, no batteries. No monthly payments and no fees;
Inflation-proof, non-taxable, In fact, it's quite relaxable;

It can't be stolen, won't pollute, One size fits all, do not dilute.
It uses little energy, But yields results enormously.

Relieves your tension and your stress, Invigorates your happiness;
Combats depression, makes you beam, It elevates your self-esteem!

Your circulation it corrects, Without unpleasant side effects.
It is, I think, the perfect drug. May I prescribe, my friend, the hug!

(And, of course, fully returnable!)

N
O
V

234

TODAY...   *I find JOY in my habit to*
SHOW A POSITIVE ATTITUDE

Worrying is sometimes like having a bulldog on the end of a rag – you can't shake it lose no how, and it's even worse if you're trying to fall asleep. When a worry comes into your mind today, counteract it with a positive thought or with the thought of an action you can take to ease the situation.

> *Blessed is the person who is too busy to worry in the daytime and too sleepy to worry at night.*
> LEO AIKMAN

What's the use of worrying? It never was worthwhile,
So pack up your troubles in your old kit-bag, and smile, smile, smile.
GEORGE ASAF (GEORGE H. POWELL), PACK UP YOUR TROUBLES IN YOUR OLD KIT-BAG

It's always darkest —
just before I open my eyes.

22
November
23

Show a P☺sitive ATTITUDĒ *in November*

𝕲𝖔𝖑𝖉𝖊𝖓 𝕽𝖚𝖑𝖊 Habit

TODAY...   *I find JOY in my habit to*
SHOW A POSITIVE ATTITUDE

Blessings are the antithesis of worries. November is when we celebrate our blessings with thanksgiving. Oprah Winfrey suggests to keep your mind on blessings instead of worries by keeping a "Grateful Journal" near your bedside. Every night before going to sleep, write down in the Journal, at least five blessings that you are grateful for, that day.

> *Blessings brighten while we count them.* MALTHIE D. BABCOCK

> *Better to lose count while naming your blessings*
> *than to lose your blessings by counting your troubles.*
> MALTHIE D. BABCOCK

> *Not what we say about our blessings, but how we use them*
> *is the true measure of our thanksgiving.*
> W.T. PURKISER

Bees hum because — *they don't know the words.*

N
O
V

TODAY...   *I find JOY in my habit to*
SHOW A POSITIVE ATTITUDE

A positive attitude may not solve your problems,
but it will annoy enough people to make it worth the effort.
HERM ALBRIGHT

The best way to pay for a lovely moment is to enjoy it.
RICHARD BACH, THE BRIDGE ACROSS FOREVER

If you are happy, you can always learn to dance.
BALINESE SAYING

If you can't stand the heat — *go swimming.*

Golden Rule Habit — Show a Positive Attitude in November — November 24 25

TODAY...   *I find JOY in my habit to*
SHOW A POSITIVE ATTITUDE

In this overly busy world we share, it's gotten too easy to become too serious about everything. Our "forgotten youth" and its merriment, gets lost in the conservative effort to be an "adult." There's a great phrase for this – "Lighten UP!!"

Destroy your conservative reputation, laugh uproariously today.
DANNY KAYE

Everybody's got a laughing place. Trouble is....
most folks won't take time to go look for it!
BRIAR RABBIT, UNCLE REMUS, "SONG OF THE SOUTH" ROBB SAGENDORPH

The most wasted day of all is that on which we have not laughed.
SEBASTIEN ROCH NICOLAS CHAMFORT

N
O
V

Don't waste today — *laugh and the world will laugh with you.*

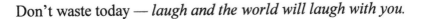

236

TODAY . . .   ***I find JOY in my habit to***
SHOW A POSITIVE ATTITUDE

A Smile
WISDOM FROM THE INTERNET

Smiling is infectious, you catch it like the flu.
When someone smiled at me today, I started smiling too.

I passed around the corner, and someone saw my grin –
When he smiled I realized, I'd passed it on to him.

I thought about that smile, then I realized its worth,
A single smile, just like mine, could travel round the earth.

So, if you feel a smile begin, don't leave it undetected –
Let's start an epidemic quick, and get the world infected!

Smile — and the world smiles with you.

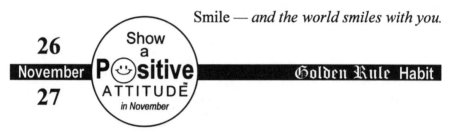

26
November
27

Show a Positive Attitude in November

𝕲𝖔𝖑𝖉𝖊𝖓 𝕽𝖚𝖑𝖊 Habit

TODAY . . .   ***I find JOY in my habit to***
SHOW A POSITIVE ATTITUDE

Here are some more uplifting quotes about smiles. I thought I'd really concentrate on smiles since it is close to the end of the month and the more you have, the more they will carry on into December and the new year. Smiles carry their own message – SMILE often.

A warm smile is the universal language of kindness.
WILLIAM ARTHUR WARD, "REWARD YOURSELF"

A smile is the chosen vehicle for all ambiguities.
HERMAN MELVILLE, AMERICAN AUTHOR

Smiles are the soul's kisses.
MINNA ANTRIM, NAKED TRUTH AND VEILEDALLUSIONS

A smile is the beginning of peace.
MOTHER TERESA

N O V

TODAY . . .   I find JOY in my habit to
SHOW A POSITIVE ATTITUDE

Life goes by at such a fast pace, we sometimes get so caught up in our own affairs that we forget to really care about others. It's an odd thing to say, but if you think about it – it is often true. This is what happens when we are not listening to another person because we are thinking about what our own response will be. Or are thinking about what we want from them, instead of what they need from us. Try expanding your life in a healthy way by jumping into the point of view of someone else today.

> *You can make your world so much larger*
> *simply by acknowledging everyone else's.*
> JEANNE MARIE LASKAS

A rolling stone — *plays the guitar.*

𝔊olden 𝔕ule Habit   Show a P☺sitive ATTITUDE in November   **28** November **29**

TODAY . . .   I find JOY in my habit to
SHOW A POSITIVE ATTITUDE

Mary Poppins popularized the "spoonful of sugar" approach to encouraging others. When you want someone in your life to change, there are many ways to work on it. Many people use anger, and never realize that anger rarely causes inspired positive changes in anyone.

A pat on the back is only a few inches away from a kick in the pants, but it is miles ahead in getting results.
V. WILCOX

> *You can't give people pride, but you can provide the kind of*
> *understanding that makes people look to their inner strengths*
> *and find their own sense of pride.*
> CHARLESZETTA WADDLES

N O V

The squeaking wheel gets — *annoying.*

TODAY . . .   *I find JOY in my habit to*
SHOW A POSITIVE ATTITUDE

Sometimes it doesn't make sense to suggest that we have to practice having a positive attitude. We practice everything else, from the multiplication tables to tricep lifts on the weight bar. I have read studies about how people have actually "learned" to become more optimistic. Make an effort from now on to check out your thinking when you get on a negative jag and practice having a positive thought about the person or event that is getting you down.

Happiness is a thing to be practiced,
— like the violin.
JOHN LUBBOCK

30
November

Things turn out the best
for people who make the best
of the way things turn out.
ART LINKLETTER

Let's close our November inspirations on a jovial note. Here are a few more quotes about laughter. With the Holiday season ahead, you'll be glad you worked on practicing a positive attitude this month.

It's bad to hold in laughter.
It goes back down inside and spreads to your hips.
FRED ALLEN

Laughter
...the most civilized music in the world.
SIR PETER USTINOV, BRITISH ACTOR, DEAR ME

N
O
V

He who laughs — LASTS.
AUTHOR UNKNOWN

CHAPTER 12

Color "Cue" - EVER-Green

"Together We Can Brighten the World We All Share."

240

Give a gift of the *Golden Rule Revolution* to the people in your life.
For quantity pricing see the card at the back of this book. If someone else has used this form, you may phone: 724-453-0447 e.mail: allofus@icubed.com or visit our website: www.goldenrulerevolution.com

IN DECEMBER, REMEMBER TO...
CELEBRATE COMMUNITY, FAMILY & FRIENDS

December is the last month of the calendar year. This great month of Holidays gives me a chance to celebrate you – my readers and friends. December's celebration color is "EVER-Green." Whenever I see an evergreen tree, I am reminded of the constancy of relationships throughout our lives. In caring relationships, we turn moments into memories. Whether finely-seamed or tattered and torn, relationships are the fabric threads that connect us to one another.

In December, while we celebrate in the spirit of our Holidays, the warm feeling of peace on earth is the strongest. The famous historian Will Durant once said, *"Civilization is just the slow process of learning to be kind."* I guess the question then is – just how well have we learned to be kind?

Imagine how we will feel one day – when peace on earth really comes true. Imagine no violence, no child abuse, no poverty, no hunger and no war. Cherish kindness. Celebrate your relationships with others this month. Use your 1,440 minutes each day, to let them know you care.

Goal for the month:

Let there be peace on earth and let it begin with me.

"Together We Can Brighten the World We All Share."

Written with a Pen...
BY PAUL HARVEY

We tried so hard to make things better for our kids that we might
have made them worse. For my grandchildren, I'd like better.

I'd really like for them to know about hand-me down clothes
and homemade ice cream and leftover meatloaf sandwiches.

I hope they learn humility by being humiliated, and learn honesty
by being cheated. I hope they learn to make their beds
and mow the lawn and wash the car.

And, my cherished grandchild, I really hope nobody gives you a
brand new car when you are sixteen. I hope you have a job by then.

It will be good if at least one time you can see a baby calf born
and your old dog put to sleep.

I hope you have to share a bedroom with your younger brother.
It's all right to draw a line down the middle of the room.

When you want to see a Disney movie and your little brother
wants to tag along, I hope you'll let him.

I hope you have to walk uphill to school with your friends
and that you live in a town where you can do it safely.

I hope you learn to dig in the dirt and read books.
When you learn to use those newfangled computers,
I hope you also learn to add and subtract in your head.

I hope you get razzed by your friends when you have your
first crush on a girl, and when you talk back to your mother
that you learn what Ivory soap tastes like.

May you skin your knee climbing a mountain, burn your hand
on a stove and get your tongue stuck on a frozen flagpole.

I sure hope you make time to sit on a porch with your grandpa
and go fishing with your uncle. May you feel sorrow at a funeral
and the joy of holidays.

I hope your mother punishes you for throwing a baseball through a
window and that she hugs and kisses you when you give her a
plaster of Paris mold of your hand.

These things I wish for you – tough times and disappointment,
hard work and above all, happiness.

TODAY . . .   *I love my habit to* **CELEBRATE**
             COMMUNITY, FAMILY & FRIENDS

Start this month with thoughts that focus on your family.
Take an audit.
How is your marriage, your parenting, your sibling relationships
and your own role as the child?
Where can you do better – how might you change your priorities?

> *Other things may change us,*
> *but we start and end with the family.*
> ANTHONY BRANDT

CELEBRATE: A renewal of family.

Golden Rule Habit | Celebrate COMMUNITY, FAMILY & FRIENDS™ in December | **1** December **2**

TODAY . . .   *I love my habit to* **CELEBRATE**
             COMMUNITY, FAMILY & FRIENDS

I heard a joke the other day – that what most people make best for
dinner these days is "reservations." We live in a fast-paced society –
it's way too easy to get on the fast track ourselves. Step down off the
track for a moment today – especially if you are a parent. How's your
"loving involvement" doing? What will you change?

> *"Home cooking," is something a lot of families are not.*
> AUTHOR UNKNOWN

> *A sense of belonging, the loving involvement of parents*
> *which creates a sense of worth, and a sense of purpose*
> *are what every child deserves to receive.*
> CYRIL J. BARBER

CELEBRATE: Prepare a meal and eat together at home tonight.

DEC

TODAY . . .   *I love my habit to* **CELEBRATE COMMUNITY, FAMILY & FRIENDS**

Focus on spending time with loved ones.

The best inheritance a parent can give his children,
is a few minutes of his time each day.

O.A. BATTISTA

Spare the rod and spoil the child – that is true.
But besides the rod, keep an apple to give him
when he has done well.

MARTIN LUTHER, GERMAN THEOLOGIAN

CELEBRATE: Think about the best family meal you can remember.
Was the food good?

3

December   **Celebrate COMMUNITY, FAMILY & FRIENDS** in December   **Golden Rule Habit**

4

TODAY . . .   *I love my habit to* **CELEBRATE COMMUNITY, FAMILY & FRIENDS**

Examine the question, *"How do you make a habit out of loving relationships?"* What is the quality of "more than friendship"?

Mummy herself has told us that she looked upon us
more as her friends than her daughters.
Now that is all very fine, but still, a friend can't take
a mother's place. I need my mother as an example
which I can follow. I want to be able to respect her.

ANNE FRANK, THE DIARY OF A YOUNG GIRL

One has to grow up with good talk in order to form the habit of it.

HELEN HAYES, AMERICAN ACTRESS, A GIFT OF JOY

D
E
C

CELEBRATE: Spend an hour listening.

TODAY...   *I love my habit to* **CELEBRATE**
                         COMMUNITY, FAMILY & FRIENDS

Setting a good example for children is a win/win effort. Exemplary behavior improves our own lives and sense of self-worth, too. We know children are astonishingly perceptive. Parenting "How-to" courses won't help us to create healthy well-adjusted children unless we show children good examples in our own lives. I call it "being our best-self."

> *A child is not likely to find a father in God*
> *until he finds something of God in his father.*
> AUSTIN L. SORENSEN

Children don't want to be told; they want to be shown.
It takes years of telling to undo one unwise showing.
EILEEN M. HAASE

CELEBRATE: Show someone
your "best self" today.

Celebrate COMMUNITY, FAMILY & FRIENDS in December

5

Golden Rule Habit   December

6

TODAY...   *I love my habit to* **CELEBRATE**
                         COMMUNITY, FAMILY & FRIENDS

Mutual respect is the essence of the Golden Rule. I also think mutual respect is the essence of good parenting. All to often – respect for a child's dignity and worth, gets lost in our outbursts of anger and criticism.

> *It is etiquette for a son or daughter to talk to the father*
> *in a gentle and polite tone, and the parent, except when*
> *reprimanding or correcting his children, is required*
> *by custom to reciprocate the compliment in the same*
> *way as his children extend it to him.*
> JOMO KENYATTA, ON GIKUYU CUSTOM

CELEBRATE: The dignity of children. Balance criticism with praise.

D E C

246

TODAY... *I love my habit to* **CELEBRATE COMMUNITY, FAMILY & FRIENDS**

My own childhood was like "trying to grow up in the display window of a furniture store." My mom had a Bachelor of Science in Home Economics and not one mess was ever allowed – anywhere in the house at all – period. When I saw this quote by Phyllis Diller, I called mom immediately and said, *"Here's one for you!"*

> *Cleaning your house while your kids are still growing*
> *is like shoveling the walk before it stops snowing.*
> PHYLLIS DILLER, ACTRESS-COMEDIENNE

CELEBRATE: Make a big mess.

7 December 8 — **Celebrate COMMUNITY, FAMILY & FRIENDS™** *in December* — **Golden Rule Habit**

TODAY... *I love my habit to* **CELEBRATE COMMUNITY, FAMILY & FRIENDS**

Another quality, too often lost in today's fast-paced world, is that of AWE and our sense of the sacred. Look into the face of a child. Know that you are looking at the miracle of creation and our hope for the future of the world.

> *Every child comes with the message*
> *that God is not yet discouraged of man.(woman)*
> RABINDRANATH TAGORE, STRAY BIRDS

DEC

CELEBRATE: Tuck someone into bed tonight.

TODAY . . .   *I love my habit to* **CELEBRATE**
                  COMMUNITY, FAMILY & FRIENDS

Our family is our own personal "hardy" EVER-green. Its shape or form doesn't matter. Whether our family is a nuclear unit, an extended step-family, blood related, adopted or by choice...once formed, with love, family weathers any storm.

> *The family is a community of persons and the smallest social unit. It is the cradle of life and love, the place in which the individual is born and grows.*
>
> POPE JOHN PAUL II, "LETTER TO FAMILIES"

Family faces are magic mirrors. Looking at people
who belong to us, we see the past, present and future.
        GAIL LUMET BUCKLEY

CELEBRATE: Remember and cherish your most recent hug.

Golden Rule Habit   Celebrate COMMUNITY, FAMILY & FRIENDS™ in December   **9** December **10**

TODAY . . .   *I love my habit to* **CELEBRATE**
                  COMMUNITY, FAMILY & FRIENDS

What is the definition of "home"?
Is it just the place we sleep and where we spend most of our time, or is home more than that?
Is the home of a friend or family member our home too?

> *Home is the place where, when you have to go there,*
> *they have to take you in.*
>
> ROBERT FROST, AMERICAN POET, "DEATH OF THE HIRED MAN"

> *In prosperity, our friends know us;*
> *in adversity, we know our friends.*
>
> JOHN CHURTON COLLINS

CELEBRATE: The meaning of home.

D E C

TODAY...   *I love my habit to* **CELEBRATE**
COMMUNITY, FAMILY & FRIENDS

What is important to you about being a parent? You have probably heard the saying that "We owe our children only roots and wings." Sometimes we forget that the heritage of our earth is part of what we owe our children. Clean air and water and a thriving ecosystem is the only way to insure their passage into a healthy future.

> *We have not inherited the earth from our ancestors*
> *we are borrowing it from our children.*
> AUTHOR UNKNOWN

Every child born into this world belongs to the whole human race.
GREER GARSON, IRISH ACTRESS, "BLOSSOMS IN THE DUST" (1941)

CELEBRATE: Make the earth a part of December's celebration.
Recycle or walk instead of drive.

11
December   **Celebrate COMMUNITY, FAMILY & FRIENDS™** *in December*   𝕲𝖔𝖑𝖉𝖊𝖓 𝕽𝖚𝖑𝖊 Habit
12

TODAY...   *I love my habit to* **CELEBRATE**
COMMUNITY, FAMILY & FRIENDS

Friendship is as old as society itself. Cicero was a great Roman philosopher, orator and statesman. Two thousand years ago, in letters to his brother and friends, Cicero shared with them – and with us – the philosophy of stoicism and life that we know today.

> *Friendship adds a brighter radiance to prosperity and*
> *lightens the burden of adversity by dividing and sharing it.*
> • • •
> *Friendship is nothing else than an accord in all things,*
> *human and divine, enjoined with mutual good will and affection,*
> *and I am inclined to think that, with the exception of wisdom,*
> *no better thing has been given to man.*
> CICERO

D
E
C

CELEBRATE: Write a letter to a friend.

TODAY . . .   *I love my habit to* **CELEBRATE COMMUNITY, FAMILY & FRIENDS**

It's the holiday season and a time when stress can build up and cause friction between family and friends. The holidays are about joyfulness, not about having too much to do. As the old saying goes, "Keep your eye on the donut, not the hole." Keep your eyes on the people you love and not the stuff, even if the stuff is the gifts you are buying for those you love. Remember, the true gift is YOU.

Fair or foul weather, we must all stick together.
UNDERDOG, "UNDERDOG"

Treat your friends as you do your pictures,
and place them in the best possible light.
JENNIE JEROME CHURCHILL, "FRIENDSHIP" TALK ON BIG SUBJECTS

CELEBRATE: Put people ahead of stuff.

Golden Rule Habit   Celebrate COMMUNITY, FAMILY & FRIENDS™ in December   **December**   **13**   **14**

TODAY . . .   *I love my habit to* **CELEBRATE COMMUNITY, FAMILY & FRIENDS**

Make TWO lists this holiday season: first – of the gifts you plan to give and second – of the visits you plan to make to the homes of family and friends. You might visit a senior home or a volunteer center too. Once you have made your lists, begin the joyous journey.

Go oft to the house of thy friend,
for weeds choke the unused path.
RALPH WALDO EMERSON, AMERICAN AUTHOR, POET AND ESSAYIST

Fate chooses our relatives, we choose our friends.
JACQUES DELILLIE

CELEBRATE: Take time to visit a friend.

D
E
C

250

TODAY . . .   *I love my habit to* **CELEBRATE**
COMMUNITY, FAMILY & FRIENDS

I call you friends,
since I have made known to all that I have heard from my Father.
It was not you who chose Me, it was I who chose you
to go forth and bear fruit.

BIBLE, JOHN 15: 15-16

My friends are my wealth.

EMILY DICKINSON, POET

I never met a man (person) I didn't like.

WILL ROGERS, AMERICAN HUMORIST

CELEBRATE: The wealth you chose for yourself.

15
December
16

Celebrate COMMUNITY, FAMILY & FRIENDS™ in December

Golden Rule Habit

TODAY . . .   *I love my habit to* **CELEBRATE**
COMMUNITY, FAMILY & FRIENDS

What is friendship? We all have friendships that ebb and flow. Some-times we see friends frequently and sometimes months go by with no contact. We call them friends, because we know that they can be counted on to be there for us, and vice versa, if needed. That's why I've often thought that the difference between a "fair weather friend," and a "foul weather friend," is more than the weather.

A true friend is someone who is there for you
when he'd rather be somewhere else.

LEN WEIN

Friendship is neither a formality nor a mode:
it is rather a way of life.

DAVID GRAYSON

CELEBRATE: Give up something to be there for a friend.

D
E
C

TODAY . . . **I love my habit to CELEBRATE
COMMUNITY, FAMILY & FRIENDS**

As you go through your day; in meetings, at your desk or workstation, in classrooms, family rooms and the grocery store, look around you. Every person you see is a friend or family member to someone, some-where – and every person is part of the meaning in the lives of one another. As far as I'm concerned, every single person is important.

Friendship is the only cement that will hold the world together.
DUKE ELLINGTON, AMERICAN MUSICIAN

*How rare and wonderful is that flash of a moment
when we realize we have discovered a friend.*
WILLIAM ROTSLER

CELEBRATE: Appreciate the friends we already know and those we are about to discover.

17

Golden Rule Habit — **Celebrate COMMUNITY, FAMILY & FRIENDS™** *in December* — December

18

TODAY . . . **I love my habit to CELEBRATE
COMMUNITY, FAMILY & FRIENDS**

If you own a pet, or have walked down the pet supplies aisle at the grocery store recently, then you probably understand that pets give us something we need. They give us the kind of unquestionable, totally accepting love that we yearn for in our relationships with people. If there were a synonym for love, I would suggest the word "acceptance."

*We give them the love we can spare,
the time we can spare.
In return, dogs have given us their absolute all.
It is without a doubt, the best deal man has ever made.*
ROGER CARAS, PRESIDENT, A.S. P.C.A., A CELEBRATION OF DOGS

CELEBRATE: Acceptance as your definition for love.

D
E
C

252

TODAY . . .   *I love my habit to* **CELEBRATE**
 COMMUNITY, FAMILY & FRIENDS

Just say, "I'll be there." Being there for a friend is the greatest gift we can give. When we help others – healthy things happen to them and to us. We are renewed in love and our spirits soar.

When you face a crisis, you know who your true friends are.
EARVIN "MAGIC" JOHNSON, LOS ANGELES LAKERS

Winter, spring, summer or fall,
All you have to do is call,
And I'll be there.
You've got a friend.
CAROLE KING, AMERICAN SINGER-COMPOSER, "YOU'VE GOT A FRIEND"

CELEBRATE: Practice saying, "I'll be there."

19
December

20

Celebrate COMMUNITY, FAMILY & FRIENDS™ in December

𝔊𝔬𝔩𝔡𝔢𝔫 𝔕𝔲𝔩𝔢 Habit

TODAY . . .   *I love my habit to* **CELEBRATE**
 COMMUNITY, FAMILY & FRIENDS

Are you a "masterpiece" friend and a "garden of delight"? We all grow up with our garden of weeds; a short temper, impatience with others, a tendency to self-absorption, an inability to listen – we each have our own embarrassing list. But as we become more aware of our weeds, and how they affect others, we can prune the thorns, cut the dead wood and clear and plant the seeds of consideration and compassion.

An old friend can be a garden of true delight.
NICK BEILENSON

A friend may well be reckoned the masterpiece of nature.
RALPH WALDO EMERSON, AMERICAN POET, AUTHOR AND ESSAYIST

CELEBRATE: Pick a fault (like not listening) and start hacking away at it!

TODAY . . .   *I love my habit to* **CELEBRATE COMMUNITY, FAMILY & FRIENDS**

This is the time of year when peace and love are in the air. It's a good time to grab 'hold of the spirit of love and make a resolution to keep that spirit going.

> *It is change that makes the world go round*
> *– but it's love that keeps it populated.*
> CHARLES H. BROWER

> *Everything in the household runs smoothly*
> *when love oils the machinery.*
> WILLIAM H. (ROZY) GRIER

CELEBRATE: The spirit of peace and love.
This month we celebrate Hanukkah. Learn more about why this holiday is one of light and dedication.

Golden Rule Habit   Celebrate COMMUNITY, FAMILY & FRIENDS™ in December   **21** December **22**

TODAY . . .   *I love my habit to* **CELEBRATE COMMUNITY, FAMILY & FRIENDS**

A man who was moving to Athens asked Socrates what the Athenian people were like. Socrates asked him what people were like in his own town. The man replied that they were selfish and mean. Socrates said, *"That too, is just the kind of people you will find in Athens."* Later, another traveler asked Socrates about the people in Athens. Socrates queried him about the people in his own home town. The traveler said he missed his home full of neighbors and friends who cared for one another. Socrates then said, *"Well that's just the kind of people you will find on your way through our beautiful city of Athens."*

> *'Tis the people, not the houses that makes the city.*
> THOMAS FULLER

CELEBRATE: Knowing that your own attitude is the key.

DEC

254

TODAY...   ***I love my habit to* CELEBRATE COMMUNITY, FAMILY & FRIENDS**

The most important thing each parent (not just dads), can do for their children is to love one another. Teaching children the meaning of healthy love, and doing it by example, is critical to their growth and development. It also is a true celebration of life.

> *The most important thing a father can do for his children is to love their mother.*
>
> REV. THEODORE M. HESBURGH, FORMER PRESIDENT, NOTRE DAME

CELEBRATE: Have a "date" with your loved-one today.

23
December
24

Celebrate
COMMUNITY, FAMILY & FRIENDS™
in December

𝕲𝖔𝖑𝖉𝖊𝖓 𝕽𝖚𝖑𝖊 Habit

TODAY...   ***I love my habit to* CELEBRATE COMMUNITY, FAMILY & FRIENDS**

Do you remember the beginning of December and our quote from the famous historian Will Durant? He said, *"Civilization is just the slow process of learning to be kind."* This month of December has been a slow process of reminders about the kindness of parenting, family, friendships and love. When we focus on what's really essential – life starts to become very simple – not necessarily easy – but simple.

> *It's no use trying to be clever – we are all clever here; just try to be kind – a little kind.*
>
> F.J. FOAKES JACKSON

> *Kind words can be short and easy to speak, but their echoes are truly endless.*
>
> MOTHER TERESA, FOUNDER, MISSIONARIES OF CHARITY

D
E
C

CELEBRATE: The simplicity of kindness.

TODAY . . .   *I love my habit to* **CELEBRATE COMMUNITY, FAMILY & FRIENDS**

Today celebrates the birthday of a man of love.

> *The unity that binds us all together,*
> *that makes this earth a family,*
> *and all men brothers and the sons of God,*
> *— is love.*
>
> THOMAS WOLFE, AMERICAN AUTHOR

> *There is no surprise more magical than the surprise of being loved. It is the finger of God on one's shoulder.*
>
> CHARLES MORGAN

CELEBRATE: The "gift" of Love.

𝕲olden 𝕽ule Habit — Celebrate COMMUNITY, FAMILY & FRIENDS™ in December — **25 December 26**

TODAY . . .   *I love my habit to* **CELEBRATE COMMUNITY, FAMILY & FRIENDS**

> *The greatest gift of life is friendship.*
>
> LYNDON B. JOHNSON, 36TH PRESIDENT OF THE UNITED STATES

> *Friends are gifts you make for yourself.*
>
> DARLENE PATRICK & ELAINE PARKE

> *You don't choose your family.*
> *They are God's gift to you, as you are to them.*
>
> BISHOP DESMOND TUTU

CELEBRATE: Your "gifts" of friendship and family.

D
E
C

TODAY . . .   *I love my habit to* **CELEBRATE COMMUNITY, FAMILY & FRIENDS**

Sometimes I scratch my head and chuckle at all of us – like gerbils in a wheel – chasing the illusive something or other. I saw a satirical cartoon in the newspaper that said the new American Dream, "Me, Mine...Money." Our shared truth that we have known all along – is that LOVE, not love of money makes us happy. Love is not only free – it doesn't even exist unless you give it away.

To love others makes us happy.

KENNY "BABYFACE" EDMONDS, AMERICAN SINGER AND COMPOSER

The love you give away is the only love you keep.

ELBERT HUBBARD

Love is the glue that holds friendships together.

ANTONIO "L.A." REID, AMERICAN COMPOSER

27

December

28

CELEBRATE: LOVE.

𝔊𝔬𝔩𝔡𝔢𝔫 ℜ𝔲𝔩𝔢 Habit

TODAY . . .   *I love my habit to* **CELEBRATE COMMUNITY, FAMILY & FRIENDS**

Sometimes, holidays can feel more lonely than the rest of the year. There's a heightened sense of the "ideal" quality of love that surrounds us – on TV and during the course of festivities and family gatherings. We may think that our own lives and family are not like that. When our actual experience seems to fall short of this ideal, it feels like something that should be there – is missing. Remember, that there is no IDEAL for love – there are moments of fullness and moments of emptiness in all lives.

Love is two people...patiently feeding each other,
not one living through the soul of the other.

BESSIE HEAD

D E C

CELEBRATE: The ever-present and surprising simplicity of love.

TODAY . . .   *I love my habit to* **CELEBRATE**
                                  COMMUNITY, FAMILY & FRIENDS

Once in a while in life – we find the need to look for new friends and a new sense of community. Perhaps you are single, and have just been transferred to a new town. Perhaps you just couldn't travel back to old roots to share the holidays. One of the best ways to make new friends is to join together in giving. Participate with "friends to be" at the Salvation Army or with Habitat for Humanity or with a local worship community outreach.

There is always something left to love.
And if you ain't learned that, you ain't learned nothing.
LORRAINE HANSBERRY, AMERICAN PLAYWRIGHT

CELEBRATE: The camaraderie of giving.

Golden Rule Habit | **Celebrate COMMUNITY, FAMILY & FRIENDS** *in December* | **29** **December** **30**

TODAY . . .   *I love my habit to* **CELEBRATE**
                                  COMMUNITY, FAMILY & FRIENDS

In the midst of the holiday festivities – take time to reflect on our larger purpose. Do you believe, as I do, that every one of us is here to fulfill our own purpose in the larger plan of human brother/sisterhood? While you were replacing a light bulb, have you ever lost one of the screws that holds the light fixture together? Like the smallest screw, every one of us counts. Let there be peace on earth, and let it begin with me.

Human brotherhood* is not just a goal.
It is a condition on which our way of life depends.
Our question is whether we have the strength and the will to make
the brotherhood of man the guiding principle of our daily lives.
JOHN F. KENNEDY, 35TH PRESIDENT OF THE UNITED STATES

(*sisterhood)

CELEBRATE: Our place in the world.

D E C

TODAY . . . **I love my habit to CELEBRATE**
COMMUNITY, FAMILY & FRIENDS

Tonight, we will celebrate the coming of the New Year.

Of all the days of the year, today is when the future is a great part of our awareness.

What are your New Year's Resolutions?
How many are about family, friends and neighbors and
how many are about professional success and material goals?

> *As man* increased his knowledge of the heavens,*
> *why should he fear the unknown on earth?*
> *As man draws nearer to the stars,*
> *why should he not also draw nearer to his neighbor?(*woman)*

LYNDON B. JOHNSON, 36TH PRESIDENT OF THE UNITED STATES

31
December

Celebrate
COMMUNITY,
FAMILY &
FRIENDS™
in December

Golden Rule REVOLUTION
POSTSCRIPT

> *We have committed the Golden Rule to memory;*
> *— let us now commit it to life.*
> AUTHOR UNKNOWN

> *Our grand business is not to see what lies dimly at a distance,*
> *but to do what lies clearly at hand.*
> THOMAS CARLYLE

> *Community is not a place.*
> *Community lives in the mind, the heart, and the spirit.*
> ELAINE PARKE

D
E
C

CELEBRATE: The New Year with peace on earth and goodwill to all.

Dear Reader,

You may have started this book at any place during the year. Now, together, we are at the start of a New Year, and in the first few years of the third millennium. The coming of this millennium was billed as a great and momentous event.

Was it?

Is it?

What IS an event?

What is the idea of time?...How do we measure it and spend it?...What does it mean?...and How does it add up in our own lives?

Through the years, I have learned from the joys and from my many mistakes, that life is like a giant bag of M&Ms. What are the M&Ms? They are our "Moments" and our "Memories."

I heard a quote that describes the relationship between moments and memories with a profound essence I have never heard before. The quote is simply a call to:

Make the kind of memories that you can live with
— the rest of your life.

How profound a thought that is – how different the world would be if we lived the time we had, with the memories we are making in mind. How many divorces would there be, or bank robberies, or abused children? Would we use drugs that confuse and obliterate memories, if we had nothing in our past that we wanted to forget?

As some know and some never learn, the essence of life itself is somewhere in time and in spirit – more than in material goods. We still have trouble believing this – even though we are given examples of its truth from time to time. The life of Princess Diana was such an example. What material goods could she ever have wanted for, and yet, she wrote about being unfulfilled. She had only just begun her search for a meaningful life when it was taken away.

One of the reminder slogans I have used in this book, JOIN THE GOLDEN RULE REVOLUTION, is "Use the Magic POWER of your own 1,440." Most people ask, *"What does this mean?"* because they have never calculated the number of minutes we all have each day, to discover 1,440 minutes of power. No one has any more or any less, no matter who they are.

What a wonderful empowering thought it is, to know that we are all equal when it comes to the power we have, to use our time wisely and use it well. More than money, time has become the essential commodity of the new millennium. Take the time to read the Voice of the Millennium that follows and see if you agree. We all have the power to make moments into lasting memories to cherish. We all have the same amount of time to give and to love, to bring alive in our moments – the gifts of service and creativity that we all were born with.

Let us begin the years of this new millennium with a renewed sense of spirit. Let us commit to use the power of our time, to nourish the joy of our own memory building, and for the good of others – whether for family, friends, or for making strangers into the friends we haven't yet met.

In the Spirit of ALL of US,

Elaine

"Together We Can Brighten the World We All Share."

Voice of the Millennium
– *The Paradox of Our Age*

AUTHOR UNKNOWN

We have taller buildings, but shorter tempers.
We have wider freeways, but narrower viewpoints.
We spend more, but have less.
We buy more, but enjoy less.

We have bigger houses, but smaller families.
We have more conveniences, but less time.
We have more degrees, but less sense.
We have more knowledge, but less judgment.

We have more experts, but fewer solutions.
We have more medicines, but less well-being.
We have infinite ends, but limited means.

We spend so recklessly, laugh so little, drive so fast,
get angry so quickly, stay up too late, get up too tired,
read seldom, watch TV too much, and pray not enough.

We have multiplied our possessions, but reduced our values.
We talk too much, love too seldom and lie too often.
We've learned how to make a living, but not a life.
We have added years to life, not life to years.

We have been all the way to the moon and back, but
have trouble crossing the street to meet the new neighbor.
We've conquered outer space, but not inner space.
We have done larger things, but not better things.

262

We've cleaned up the air, but polluted the souls.
We've split the atom, but not our prejudice.
   We write more, but learn less.
   We plan more, but accomplish less.

We have learned to rush, but not to wait.
We have higher incomes, but lesser earnings.
   We have more food, but less satisfaction.
   We have more acquaintances, but fewer friends.

We make more effort, but succeed less.
We are long on quantity, short on quality.
   We act smart, instead of being smart.
   We have fancier houses, but broken homes.

These are the times of world peace, but domestic warfare,
   more leisure and less fun;
   more kinds of food, but less nutrition.

This is a time when there is much in the show window,
   and nothing in the stockroom.

What a life if full of care,
   We have no time to stand and stare.

(Dear Reader - between late 1999 and the early weeks of 2000, I received six copies of this Millennium Voice on my e.mail from six different friends. It seemed worth sharing to them and so I am sharing it with you. It's not a pretty picture. I hope the GOLDEN RULE REVOLUTION will help. Thank you to the person who wrote and shared this powerful message.)

CONCLUSION and NEW BEGINNINGS

This is NOT the end of this book. It may be 365 days later than the day you purchased it or received it from a friend or family member, but it is NOT the end of the Golden Rule Celebration for you, or of the Revolution for all of us.

We have been buying Ford automobiles for nearly 100 years and McDonald's fast foods for more than 30 years. If we keep reminding ourselves of the Golden Rule, the way they remind us of their products – the GOLDEN RULE REVOLUTION can succeed and be sustained forever.

The first most important idea I shared with you at the beginning was that the Golden Rule is universal and includes us all. The second most important idea I want to share with you is that the end of this book is a BEGINNING, not an end. Just like all holidays return every year, together, day after day, month after month, year after year, we can celebrate each habit again and again. The monthly Golden Rule Habits can return every year to your life and to the lives of us all. Let's live the Golden Rule Habits and re-discover the sense of awe and sacred wonder of childhood.

> *Life is the childhood of our immortality.*
> GOERTHE

The GOLDEN RULE REVOLUTION was prepared for you as a simple, practical book about what a fulfilled and enriched way of life has always meant to me. It is a book to bring us back to the "forgotten shreds of simplicity in our quiet hearts." It is a new chapter in the rally of our shared human spirit that is bursting to be set free. This is a RALLY of what we have in common – the need to give and to receive love, appreciation and respect.

There is no complete panacea because we all have free will. However, think about this for a minute. What a great win/win/win/win/win/win we will all share together – when the Golden Rule becomes more than the greatest concept ever known. Think about what life will be like when the Golden Rule becomes powerful beyond measure.

Our own lives will be enriched beyond measure.
Our marriages or committed relationships will be strengthened.
Our families will be stronger and happier.
Our children will thrive.
Our work environment will be a place of joy and personal fulfillment.
Productivity will multiply as interpersonal problems diminish.
Our earth will be valued as the one thing we all share.
Air and water will be cleaner, there will be less litter, and less waste.
There will be fewer hungry people – or people without homes.
There will be fewer fights and fewer wars.
There will be more smiles.
There will be fewer frowns.
There will be more peace and tranquility.
And...
And.................................
And.............The possibilities are endless.

Before ending this book I want to share one personal story. Since I began this journey in 1987, to bring the Golden Rule more alive among us, I have met many people, young and old, across the country and internationally. However, I will never forget one Professor at Carnegie Mellon University in Pittsburgh, Pennsylvania. He inquired and expressed curiosity about my (then) school project, The Caring Habit of the Month Adventure.

I explained to him my caring habit concept with animated enthusiasm and my three points; (1) everything will get better if we all treat each other better, (2) the repetitive principles of media are powerful, habit-forming and they reach everyone, (3) each person is important and our daily actions have more influence on life than we realize.

Eventually, when I paused for a few moments to catch my breath, I noticed a twinkle in his eye as he folded his arms over his belly and slowly looked down over his professorial half-glasses. Then he said, *"Let me see if I understand you, Elaine. You want everyone to be nice to each other...so you're just going to keep pestering us until we all start doing it."*

Yes I am guilty of wanting to "pester people" until more of us practice kindness and compassion more often than ever before. Rarely, have I been blessed with a better opportunity to chuckle at myself. Thank you Professor Baumann, wherever you are.

THANK YOU

Thank you for joining with me in this GOLDEN RULE REVOLUTION. I hope your new beginning has been joyous and fulfilling. I would love to hear stories about your adventures and celebrations, and what has changed for you because of the Golden Rule journey you are now on.

AND remember, to keep the GOLDEN RULE REVOLUTION going in your life.

It is not ever, ever, ever meant to end.

GRATEFUL ACKNOWLEDGMENTS

Writing this book has been a caring adventure, filled with gifts of self from many cherished people. Most of all, I want to thank the children in Aliquippa, Pennsylvania, who proved to me that caring and excellence can become more popular than self-centeredness.

I also want to thank all of the great hearts around the world, old and young, past and present whose wise quotes grace these pages. Every credit we could find is listed. To those contributing sages whose names we couldn't find – THANK YOU IN SPIRIT.

I as a writer, and you as a reader, owe a special thank you to Darlene Patrick. Her illustrative gifts come from her heart and without her, the Caring Habit school program, and this book, wouldn't be possible. She is also, and best of all, a dedicated mom to 3 beautiful children.

JOIN THE GOLDEN RULE REVOLUTION would not be here in your hands without my "encouragers," the people who just wouldn't let me fail to achieve this dream... no matter how loudly I protested. My "defining" encourager in life was my grandfather, George A. Spies. My example of quiet volunteerism and service was my dad. Also, to Albert Marks, a special thank you.

Just a few of the encouragers and participants to whom I am also indebted are: my sons, my mother, my sister, my life-long best friend, Kay Peters, Rev. David W. Abbott, Dr. Dennis Afton, Karin Allen, Becky Barron, Vince Blackwell, Dr. Thomas Boslooper, Cindy Breen, Helen Britt, Kay Brown, Geoffrey Bullington, Miriam Cherin, Renny Clark, Harold Cooper, Jeane & Jimmy Dunn, Herb & Joan Eye, Erik Falck, Connie & Pat Flaugher, Jan Getz, Karen Gibson, Linda & Andy Godek, Aunt Budge Grover, Tracy Heinlein, Dr. Randall Henion, Rev. Doug Hill, Kathleen Isaacs, Deborah Kaiser, Dr. Alison Kallman, Jeff Kimmel, David & Heather Klenovich, Cheryl Kubelick, Kacey Locke, John Looney, Dr. Judith McQuaide, Mary Ann Moran, Ralph Moore, Dawn Mowad, Luci & Perry Newton, Betsy & Pam Nettelbeck, Peggy Nowicki, Myra Olynik, Ernie Panza, Jeff Patrick, Kaaren Radecki, Dr. Francis Rogers, MeMe Schimmel, Honorable Judge William T. Simmons, Louise Slaughter, Eileen Smith, Mort & Judith Stanfield, Dr. Melvin & Adrena Steals, Rob Stemple, and Aaron Walton.

Thank you, thank you, one and all.

The future of the GOLDEN RULE REVOLUTION will be written, **NOT** by Elaine Parke, *but by **YOU**!*

Please . . .

• Share your stories about Golden Rule people and happenings in your community.

• Send us your ideas for making your own "Golden Rule" habit-building reminders.

• Write Golden Rule music, raps, poetry, stories and drama or create artwork to symbolize Golden Rule qualities.

• Send in your suggestions and ideas that can help strengthen this GOLDEN RULE REVOLUTION of kindness, compassion and mutual respect.

HOW TO CONTACT THE AUTHOR

Mrs. Parke provides consulting services, schools, workshops and seminars for businesses, associations, social agencies, and non-profit organizations nationwide. Your inquiries, stories, habit-building reminder ideas, and other suggestions should also be directed to Elaine or Darlene Patrick at the address below. We look forward to hearing from you.

Elaine Parke or Darlene Patrick
Box 561
Zelienople, PA 16063

ABOUT THE AUTHOR

Elaine Stevens Parke was just 19, when she volunteered as a reading tutor for Racketeer, Cobra and Vice-Lord gang kids on Chicago's North Side. In August 1961, TIME Magazine reported on her work and concerns about the frustrating limitations of "one-person-at-a-time" social solutions. Then, a marketing student at Northwestern University, she asked herself, *"How do we expand the scope of positive influence to reach more kids more easily?"* Her first response was to spend twenty-five years fine tuning her mass market media skills in corporate America.

Over the years, Mrs. Parke's professional advertising campaigns have reached millions of people across America. She served as VP of Marketing for a national distributor of beauty products. Elaine is "mom" to two grown sons. She holds two U.S. patents for new product design, has over 10 years experience as a gang intervention volunteer, and is trained in violence reduction and mediation procedures.

In 1990, to fulfill her dream to reach and positively influence more children, Mrs. Parke developed the Caring Habit of the Month media-based community revitalization model, while serving as Director of Marketing for a resort community. She and a team of community leaders implemented a successful pilot model in nearby Somerset, PA.

This book, JOIN THE GOLDEN RULE REVOLUTION, is based on media principles that, for ten years, she has used in communities and schools to improve the climate of caring, and work ready social skills among youth. In May, 2000, her public school Caring Habit of the Month Adventure curriculum won a Pennsylvania State Violence-FREE Youth Governor's Award. Caring Habit television public service ads have reached more than a million families daily throughout the greater Pittsburgh region.

Mrs. Parke is a consultant with "Caring MEDIA International," has published national media studies, consulted to the Catholic Church, and is an occasional Guest Marketing Lecturer for Carnegie Mellon University. She is becoming a recognized authority on the application of media and marketing principles to achieve social and educational goals. Recent articles by Mrs. Parke have appeared in publications of the National Association of School Psychologists, the National Association of Secondary School Principals, and the Educational Digest.

ABOUT THE ILLUSTRATOR

Darlene Kamauf Patrick has been a professional free-lance artist for nearly two decades. Upon graduating from the Art Institute of Pittsburgh with an Associate Degree in Specialized Technology, she began her career in a variety of design environments while she built a free-lance clientele base. Her client list includes: colleges, health club facilities, hospitals, machine manufacturers, pharmaceutical distributors, resort communities, restaurants, retail malls, telecommunication companies as well as numerous product distributors. By working with different companies throughout her career, she has enjoyed the flavors of many aspects of advertising and print production. In the last decade, she streamlined her range of expertise to focus on graphic design and corporate identity. She markets her original line of greeting cards – "the Bow-tie Collection" as well as other customized celebration ideas.

Darlene's involvement with Elaine Parke began nearly a decade ago, when she answered a classified ad calling for a free-lance artist. Since then, they have built a partnership in the development and imaging of the caring reminder system known as the 12 Monthly Habits. Her energetic style inspired the logo-like identity for each monthly theme. Her printed illustrations and graphics for The Caring Habit of the Month Adventure can be seen in many middle school environments throughout the Greater Pittsburgh region. She felt it a natural next-step to once again team-up with the author on the design and production of this book – JOIN THE GOLDEN RULE REVOLUTION. Of all the projects the artist has worked on in her career, none have been as challenging and fulfilling as working together with Elaine to inspire mutual respect and more caring between all people.

Mrs. Patrick is a graphic design consultant with "Caring MEDIA International", has won several print-media and design awards, volunteers her talents with the Girl Scouts of America as well as the Westmoreland Hospice and considers her three beautiful children her greatest work of art. Her studio is in her Greensburg, Pennsylvania home that she shares with her husband, Jeff, and their children, Heather, Ryan and Samantha.

If you would like to receive
information about future
books, tapes, lectures, etc.
by Elaine Parke
and/or
Darlene Patrick
please...

Send Your Name and Address
or for quicker response—
A #10 self-addressed stamped envelope
to
Caring Media International, Ltd.
305 Furnace Drive - Suite B
Zelienople, PA 16063

—or—

E.mail us at
allofus@icubed.com

—or—

Call 724-453-0447

Start a Golden Rule Revolution Of Your Own...

This Book makes a Great Gift!
— OR —
Use it as a Fund-Raiser for
Your School, Organization
or Place of Worship.

Mail TODAY!

Take ONE of your 1,440 minutes TODAY and Order More Copies of _Elaine Parke's_ ...

JOIN

—THE—

𝕲𝖔𝖑𝖉𝖊𝖓 𝕽𝖚𝖑𝖊

REVOLUTION

Practice One Habit . . .
Each Month of the Year

BONUS !!! Habit-Building Reminder Bookmarks are included.

- - - - - - If the tear-out order card at the back of this book is missing please use this form. - - - - - -

____**PLEASE register me** (my family) as member(s) of *The GOLDEN RULE REVOLUTION*. As the spirit of mutual respect and caring is built up and grows among us, I would like to be invited to participate in conferences, workshops, rallies & other events.

____ **I AM ordering** #_____ additional book copies at $19.95*/each copy.
____ These books are for non-profit fundraising.　　　**Book Price Total**_____

(PA Residents Only) **6½% SalesTax**_____

NOTE: To save shipping costs & unless you cannot find it locally, please purchase books from your local bookseller.

Add $5.40 for the first book **Shipping**_____
& $1.00 for each additional. **TOTAL:**_____

*Quantity Discounts: 3-5 books - $14.40/copy　6 or more - $12/copy　Case (36) - $10/copy

____**YES! I would like to learn more** about *The Caring Habit of the Month Adventure* as a youth violence prevention and social skills development project for my school.
Please make checks payable to: Caring Media International, Ltd.

Name_____

(Organization/School)_____ e.mail_____

Address_____

City _____ State_____ Zip_____ phone (   )_____